PRAISE FOR DOUGLAS GLOVER

"Douglas Glover's extended meditation on *Don Quixote, The Enamoured Knight*, is simply packed to the brim with marvelous stuff."
—Jeffrey Canton, *Quill and Quire*

"Douglas Glover is a writer of the greatest and most variegated gifts. . . . Glover is that rarest of artists, a true master in an age that needs masters desperately."
—Darin Strauss

"*The Enamoured Knight* wisely fuses two frequently doomed genres into a readable one, combining a thoroughly informed yet still readable run of literary criticism with a passionate and playful artist-on-art commentary."
—Darryl Whetter, *Globe and Mail*

"In the confines of a sentence, he can stagger your mind with insight, flush your face with outrage, double you over with amusement, or, quite simply and sharply, break your heart. Anyone who cares about storytelling, desire, or language—hell, anyone who *reads*—should be reading Douglas Glover."
—Lisa Carey

OTHER BOOKS BY DOUGLAS GLOVER

THE Enamoured KNIGHT

DOUGLAS GLOVER

DALKEY ARCHIVE PRESS

NORMAL · LONDON

Originally published in Canada by Oberon Press, 2004
Copyright © 2004 by Douglas Glover

First U.S. edition, 2005
All rights reserved

Library of Congress Cataloging-in-Publication Data available.
ISBN: 1-56478-404-5

Published with the financial assistance of the Program for Cultural Cooperation between
Spain's Ministry of Culture and United States Universities.

Partially funded by a grant from the Illinois Arts Council, a state agency.

Dalkey Archive Press is a nonprofit organization located at Milner Library
(Illinois State University) and distributed in the UK by
Turnaround Publisher Services Ltd. (London).

www.dalkeyarchive.com

Printed on permanent/durable acid-free paper and bound in
the United States of America.

CONTENTS

For my brothers Rodger and John,
knights-errant brave and true.

*"...wheresoever thou mayest be, mine thou art, and, wheresoever I am,
I must be thine"*—Don Quixote (Volume 2, Chapter 48).

Love and Books, an Introduction

Don Quixote is an extraordinarily contemporary story because it's
about the two pillars of modern life, love and books. To be precise,
it's about an impossibly romantic love and bad books. It's that
paradoxical thing, a book against books. The narrator's avowed purpose is "no other than to inspire mankind with an abhorrence of
the false and improbable stories recounted in books of chivalry."
(Volume 2, Chapter 74) Reading popular novels about knights-
errant drives Don Quixote mad. He falls in love with an imaginary
woman, an ideal woman called Dulcinea, and rides about the country on his nag Rozinante perpetrating acts of absurd violence on
innocent bystanders (not to mention windmills) in her name. Other
characters take advantage of his folly to create elaborate hoaxes and
provoke more mad antics for their own amusement. In Volume 2,
Quixote even meets people who have read Volume 1; they know
him better than he knows himself.

At a certain point, reading *Don Quixote* becomes a recipe for
vertigo. Every sentence spins on a comic axis creating multiple
ironies and subversions, blurring meaning. The novel's own bookishness, its awareness of itself as a book, punctures any illusion of
verisimilitude and tells the "truth" about itself. The text becomes
polysemous, becomes the proverbial elephant with critics grasping
at this or that element on which to pin an interpretation. The
old don is a Christian saint, a psychotic, the last true knight, or a
romantic dream-the-impossible-dream hero. *Don Quixote* is either
not a novel in the true sense, it's the first and greatest modern
novel, or it's an amazingly prescient postmodern confection simultaneously prefiguring Jacques Lacan and language theory (Quixote
will describe himself as "wounded by the edge of absence"). Vladimir Nabokov called it cruel. Dostoevsky said it was the saddest
book of all.

It stands in a meandering line of long prose stories that go back to the Classical Greeks, that is, to the beginning of written literature. Cervantes was clearly aware of his literary antecedents and models: the chivalric romance and what we call today the Greek novel, what the Greeks themselves called *erotika pathemata* or tales of suffering for love. The English word "novel" is misleading in this regard, connecting the genre with newness and modernity in a way that, say, the French word *roman* does not. The French word for novel etymologically ties the genre to the romance, medieval tales of chivalrous love and adventure which did derive historically from the Greek novel.

Cervantes' parody of the genre is next thing to a homage, or it is a homage. *Don Quixote* borrows plot, incident, character and theme from the chivalric romances it explicitly sets out to ridicule: chaste love, knightly adventures, single combats to the death, redemptive suffering, enchanters, giants, curing balsams, the raising of the dead, enchanted boats, Death itself, shape-changing, etc. In this, Cervantes initiated the hybrid pattern which more or less all novels have followed, romantic motif in a see-sawing tension with realistic effect (call it plausibility or verisimilitude). In any given work, the balance shifts between more or less realism and more or less myth-driven poetry or formalism. As Northrop Frye wrote in his essay "The Renaissance of Books,"

> There seems something inherently paradoxical about the structure of a genre of literature that avowedly imitates life. The reason is not really so hard to grasp. Life has no shape; literature has. A realistic story must get its shape from somewhere, and ultimately the only place it can get it from is romance, a form of fiction in which the story is told for its own sake. (*Spiritus Mundi: Essays on Literature, Myth, and Society*)

These formal structures and romantic motifs are in turn themselves borrowed or copied from archaic myths and rituals—rites of initiation and passage, fertility rites, sacrifice rites—bereft of the inherent belief systems which constituted their motivation and meaning, fragmented by faulty transmission and memory, jumbled and out of sequence. The fact that so much of what goes for narrative form has this mysteriously archaic quality is one of the things

8

that makes interpreting literature such an open-ended activity. We don't know the form of form or what myths mean or why stories cohere around desire. Indeed, so much of what happens in *Don Quixote*, examined in a certain light, seems dream-like and contingent, a quality which one begins to notice in all great stories (what about that white whale and Gustave Aschenbach's bacchanalian nightmare and Anna Karenina's peasant working mysteriously over a piece of iron as she jumps beneath the train?).

At the same time, as I have said, *Don Quixote* is passionately and wittily aware of itself as a book. It's full of authors, translators, typographers, critics, readers, projected books, lists of books, literary criticism, book burnings, found manuscripts, references to the published first volume in Volume 2, and spurious books. One of the books discussed (Volume 1, Chapter 6) is "the *Galatea* of Miguel de Cervantes." Quixote's friend the village curate remarks, "...that same Cervantes has been an intimate friend of mine, these many years...." Quixote even visits a publishing house and discusses the theory of literary translation with an author. Except for Sancho, the important characters in the novel are readers, and not just readers, avid readers, almost as obsessed with reading and literary debate as Quixote himself. Though every character has a particular social role or profession, we rarely see them doing their jobs; the curate never preaches, the barber never cuts anyone's hair, the student never studies; they mostly fit into the novel as readers. Several are writers as well as readers. Even the arch-criminal and donkey thief Gines de Passamonte is writing his memoirs, and the canon of Toledo in Volume 1 has a hundred pages of a chivalric romance in manuscript. Alonso Quixano himself, Alonso the Good, has flirted with the idea of writing a book.

> He, notwithstanding, bestowed great commendations on the author, who concludes his book with the promise of finishing that interminable adventure; and was more than once inclined to seize the quill, with a view to performing what was left undone; nay, he would have actually accomplished the affair, and published it accordingly, had not reflexions of greater moment employed his imagination, and diverted him from the execution of his design. (Volume 1, Chapter 1)

9

Books trigger Quixote's insanity; they set the novel's plot in motion; books provide the mental and moral template for Quixote's behaviour. It's no stretch to say the narrative becomes a dramatic meditation on reading, on the logical interplay of text, truth, fiction and meaning, and on the book as a constructed artifice and as a technology. This is signalled by the internal relativity machine of the nested narrators, the cascading points of view, the playful shifting of discourses, the formal repetition (doubling) of event and character, the self-reflexive critical passages, the inter-textual reference, the motifs of writing, publishing and reading, and, above all, the paradoxical argument against chivalric romances. Both Quixote and Sancho are haunted by their own unreality, by being characters trapped in a book, by the sense of being written by unseen hands.

The climax of this purely bookish invention is the moment when an impostor calling himself Don Quixote walks out of the pages of one book (the spurious *Second Volume of the Ingenious Gentleman Don Quixote of La Mancha: by the Licentiate Alonso Fernandez de Avellaneda of Tordesillas* published in 1614) into the pages of another book (Cervantes' own Volume 2) and goes to joust at Saragossa. In the world of *Don Quixote*, this impostor is only a character in a bad novel, yet there he is, walking about the countryside like every other *real* character, a miracle that can only take place in a book where the grammatical throw of language makes such sleight of hand possible. At this point, *Don Quixote* severs its last tie with verisimilitude, wrenching itself out of the discourse of reality into the relativity of discourses, of language, as it were, in that floaty, postmodern, post-structuralist sense of language as a self-referential system of signs. As Michel Foucault writes:

> *Don Quixote* is the first modern work of literature, because in it we see the cruel reason of identities and differences make endless sport of signs and similitudes; because in it language breaks off its old kinship with things and enters into that lonely sovereignty from which it will reappear, in its separated state, only as literature; because it marks the point where resemblance enters an age which is, from the point of view of resemblance, one of madness and imagination. Once similitude and signs are sundered from each

other, two experiences can be established and two characters appear face to face. (*The Order of Things*, 48-49)

The pathos of logos (reason or language) is that, as Plato pointed out, logos is always seeking completion in some lost unity, a unity made impossible by the symbolic nature of language itself. On one level, it's possible to construct a reading of *Don Quixote* as a narrative of the adventure of the mind seeking mythic closure with the world, as an image of the inevitably failed quest for knowledge, meaning, or the lost unity with things within the labyrinth of words. And, as it happens, the idea of sex, of love between a man and a woman, seems to offer the closest metaphorical parallel. So that on another level, the novel is a cracked love story. As the poet Anne Carson writes in *Eros the Bittersweet*,

In any act of thinking, the mind must reach across this space between known and unknown, linking one to the other but also keeping visible their difference. It is an erotic space. (*Eros the Bittersweet*, 171)

The Greeks called their novels tales of suffering for love. If they weren't about suffering for love, they wouldn't be tales. A story consists of someone wanting something and having trouble getting it. There are no stories about people who start out happy and contented, remain happy and contented throughout, and end up happy and contented. Imagine the phrase "tales of not-suffering for love" or "tales of having fun for love" or "tales of finding pleasure for love." The difference between pornography and literature is that in pornography everyone has orgasms all the time. There is no gap between desire and consummation. In literature there is always an element of frustration, displacement, delay and incompleteness (even if someone does eventually manage to have an orgasm). *Don Quixote* is the quintessential novel because it's about a man in love with a woman who doesn't exist. At the outset, Cervantes invents the limiting case.

Or put this another way: all novels are about acts of perversion. In novels, desire is resisted; characters invent roundabout or symbolic (fetishized or metonymic) means to try to satisfy desires which, in the very greatest works, invariably remain unsatisfied. *Don Quixote* is the story of a man so inhibited in his erotic life that instead of simply talking to the real woman he loves (the peasant girl Aldonza Lorenzo) he reinvents her as an ideal, imaginary, impossible sexual partner and revels in suffering for her absence. In fact, his desire is double-blocked; not only is Dulcinea imaginary, but the love Quixote pledges her is chaste (think of Tristan placing the sword between himself and Iseult as they bed down together in the forest).

The impossibility of closing the love circuit is a commonplace of lyric poetry and modern psychology (you have to *work* at love, they tell us, totally missing the point). Books, those false, misleading, ridiculous chivalric romances, suggest to Quixote a metonymic (or fetishized) solution to his state of erotic stasis, the way to bridge the unbridgeable gap between himself and his lover. He will communicate his love to Dulcinea through adventures and by sending back to her a stream of messages in the form of conquered enemies sworn to pay her homage and the rumour of public renown. Yet when he actually tries to write a letter to Dulcinea, he first can't find paper, then Sancho forgets to take the letter with him when he leaves. Finally Sancho recites a garbled oral version of the letter to the wrong recipient. (Think of other postal metaphors: Derrida's *The Postcard*, Poe's "The Purloined Letter," and the Dead Letter Office in Melville's "Bartleby the Scrivener.") Resistance, suffering, the gap, the imaginary bridge, and the fetish are central to the meaning of love because they delay or prevent the recognition of the impossibility of satisfaction. Arousal lies in the tension of ambiguity, incompletion and, ultimately, disappointment, which can only be relieved in death (hence, the poetic conceit that what desire desires is death).

Dulcinea is, in fact, imaginary. Love thrives, suffers in utter absence; the old knight's fancy projects a strange, solipsistic reflection of his own emptiness onto the empty screen: it has the look of a beautiful, smiling woman. And so, oddly enough, reason and reality can never penetrate the addled, love-sick mind of Quixote. Only another sign can disconfirm his fantasy. Entering his home village at the end of his long adventure, he hears the words, "Thou shalt never see it in all the days of thy life" and immediately applies them to his own situation. As in a dream, hounds appear chasing a hare. The hare hides, trembling, beneath Sancho's donkey. Sancho scoops it up and hands it to Quixote, who says, "Malum Signum, Malum

Signum! the hare flies, the hounds pursue, and Dulcinea does not appear." A few lines later Sancho hands Quixote the little cricket cage, image of his enchantment.

Bad sign. Evil sign. It's an amazing, beautifully poignant passage, packed with exuberant life, significance, and converging patterns: the two men limping home, the end of their journey, the boys squabbling over their cricket cage, the racing hounds, the quivering hare (Quixote, who began the novel as a hunter, knows exactly what they represent), the boys pushing in to see the hare, hunters hastening over the fields, and the distraught knight reading each disparate bit of reality as if it were a message for him alone.

Quixote's passionately bitten-off phrases contain the whole tragic poetry of semiotics. Bad sign, evil omen: the sign is a lack, desire chases its meaning; but the meaning, like the object Quixote has been pursuing through the novel, never appears. In the context of courtly poems and chivalric novels, as well as Quixote's madness, the chaste, semi-divine mistress is a fundamental symbol, a structuring principle of the discourse of reality, which is why the poems of the troubadours could be read ambiguously as referring to a real mistress, an ideal woman, or, in the Christian topos, the Virgin Mary. So that when Quixote cries out, "Evil sign!" he is announcing not just the end of his own obsessional fantasy but something far worse. "Lord mend us!" he exclaims, after being rescued from the mill race by those phantom millers, "the world is nothing but a continual warfare of opposite machinations and deceit...." (2,29) His words echo another famous literary doublet, Kurtz's "The horror! The horror!"—Kurtz also being a literary knight of dubious accomplishments. At the end of "Heart of Darkness," when Marlow returns to civilization (after imitating Kurtz's journey up country and following him to death's door), he tells a lie about what he has heard.

We love stories because they dramatize what we feel obscurely to be our own adventure, though we are almost always less focused and less heroic than the people who bear our standard in literature. It's a peculiar adventure. We deploy an inadequate tool, language, to mime the shape of the emptiness. Desire and resistance are like the fingers of a blind man touching the surface of an unseen wall. Naturally, so much pathos, impossibility and emptiness, as well as our propensity for risky, ill-advised existential experiments, is ripe

13

for comedy. The mind likes to think in antitheses (the form of the aphorism), and comedy and tragedy are just another example of that curious oscillation or flickering quality we find so often in *Don Quixote*. Aristotle says comedy grew out of phallic songs, an observation that makes me think of those Aubrey Beardsley prints of little men and satyrs strutting about with giant erect penises, hubris incarnated in the genital flesh, ripe for disappointment and detumescence (picture Quixote, on his scrawny old horse, with his broken lance, rusty armour and barber's basin helmet). Shakespeare's comedies, like so many modern Hollywood romantic comedies, end in marriage, a celebration of true love and fertility, which is the antithesis of Quixote's chaste, barren ideal.

The lesson here might be that art doesn't mime reality; it imitates possible realities. In story after story, novel after novel, authors repeat the hypothesis of desire. What happens if true love exists? What happens if it's just a bookish fantasy? What if we are alone and always will be? Literature becomes, through repetition and variation, a rich tangle of possible outcomes and suggested meanings which function as a commentary and gloss on our particular epics of desire. Without having recourse to Thanatos, hubris or Original Sin, there is still a meta-story with which we can identify, which is, perhaps, an old story about birth, procreation and death, especially death, which in image after image haunts the pages of *Don Quixote*, "gnawed by a dog's hunger," Sancho says, "that is never satisfied." Wittgenstein said that the religious feeling, belief in God, was perhaps nothing more than an expression of awe at the fact of our existence. We exist: the strange, complex story of desire begins, and simultaneously the counter-story, the vectors of conflict and resistance, start to whittle away our vital forces.

When we read we mime loss repetitively and in the process it seems to accrete meaning, the sense of being planned, fated or the will of the gods; we enjoy the sense of participating in a larger story, we experience the passion of the hero and, after, the generous perspective of pity and distance. What does come with repetition is a sense of mastery and control. This is the essence of repetition as a cognitive tool; it's the reason children play house or tennis players stand in front of ball machines endlessly hitting backhand shots. In the experience of reading, which is emotional rather than cognitive, we somehow find loss easier to bear.

RECOVERING THE TEXT:
TECHNICAL AND ANALYTICAL

"Now, cried Don Quixote, I am fully convinced of what I have on divers occasions believed; namely, that those inchanters, by whom I am persecuted, take pleasure in presenting realities to my view, and then changing and meta-morphosing them into such figures and forms as they choose to bestow: believe me, gentlemen, to me every thing that has passed appeared a true and literal concurrence of real facts...." (2,26)

A Basic Reading

Cervantes was born in 1547. He was in his mid-fifties when he published the first part, Volume 1, of *Don Quixote* (1605), a failed soldier (captured by the Turks, losing the use of one hand), abortive colonist (he applied for a job in Mexico but was turned down), a failed tax collector (briefly imprisoned for mishandling his accounts—he may have begun the novel in prison) and an unsuccessful playwright. He promised to deliver a sequel to the first part of *Don Quixote* but seems not to have taken his promise seriously, turning back to his plays and his exemplary novels and beloved pastorals. He was working very slowly on the sequel in late 1614 when someone else published a work called *Second Volume of the Ingenious Gentleman Don Quixote of La Mancha: by the Licentiate Alonso Fernandez de Avellaneda of Tordesillas*. Alonso Fernandez is a pseudonym. No-one has ever discovered who the author of the spurious second volume was (possibly someone in the circle of a rival playwright). But the threat of competition drove Cervantes to finish his own book quickly and it was published the next year. And then he died (on the same date as Shakespeare, although the Spanish and the English were using different calendars so it wasn't exactly the same day). The spurious second volume itself becomes part of the plot of Cervantes' own second volume; Don Quixote meets people who have read the book and even claim to have met the Don Quixote impostor.

Don Quixote is a novel about a 50-year-old man named Alonso Quixano, or Alonso the Good, who lives with two women, his 40-year-old housekeeper and his 20-year-old niece. He doesn't have much money, and he doesn't seem to have been married. He suffers from some kidney disorder—"imbecillity of the loins" in Smollett's translation (2,18)—that makes wearing a belt uncomfortable. Everything points to a life of genteel poverty, chastity, books and hunting. The only hint of eros prior to the opening of the novel comes in the description of Aldonza Lorenzo, the village girl who becomes, in Quixote's mind, Dulcinea del Toboso, the idealized woman of his knight-errant dream. "...an hale, buxom country wench, called Aldonza Lorenzo, who lived in the neighbourhood, and with who he had formerly been in love; though by all accounts, she never knew, nor gave herself the least concern about the matter." (1,2)

A shy, sexually inhibited, middle-aged man, who falls in love at a distance but never follows through, Quixano nevertheless is an avid reader with a passion for hyperventilating romance fiction in the form of the popular chivalric adventure novels of his time. In this, he is no different from consumer readers who moon over fantasy and romances novels today, imagining their unlived lives in the pages of their books. Like these modern readers, Quixano has imbibed a highly sublimated, romantic vision of love. It's not about negotiating sex with a tired, cranky spouse and putting the garbage out. It's about chaste devotion to ideal beauty, about knights in armour, damsels in distress, enchanters and giants. It's about proving one's love without actually consummating it. It's about fighting, risking death, even seeking death, as a sign of love.

As the novel opens, Alonso the Good suffers something like a psychotic breakdown. His habitual reading turns from passion to full-blown addiction and self-destructive obsession. For those readers who have windmills on the brain and hum "Dream the Impossible Dream" when they think of *Don Quixote*, it's helpful to review some of the language Cervantes uses to describe this mania. Quixano {my italics for emphasis}

> ...*addicted* himself to the reading of books of chivalry, which he perused with such *rapture* and application, that he not only *forgot* the pleasure of the chace, but also *utterly neglected* the management of his estate: nay to such a pass did his curiosity and *madness*, in this particular, *drive* him, that he sold many good acres of Terra Firma, to purchase books of knight-errantry, ...he would often read *from morning to night, and from night to morning again, without interruption*; till at last, the moisture of his brain being quite *exhausted with indefatigable* watching and study, he fairly *lost his wits*." (1,1)

If we concentrate on these passages alone, it would be difficult to decide if we were reading a comic novel or a very sad, slightly dated case history. Quixote's ideation is obsessive; his actions compulsive. He has delusions of grandeur, and later, with the invention of that horde of enchanters, his universe turns paranoid. He quickly loses the ability to function within the normal parameters of self-interest. In his obsessiveness, his insanity, he reminds us of many other great characters in fiction—Ahab, Anna Karenina, Emma Bovary, Kurtz, etc.—whose desires are so insistent, excessive and self-destructive as to appear crazy. Their obsessiveness, the repetitiveness of the situations in which they access their desires, gives their actions the character of fate. In certain lights, plots mimic demonic possession; something alien has taken over the minds of perfectly ordinary looking individuals and driven them to act in strangely repetitive, even ritualistic ways.

In the grip of his book-induced fantasy, the middle-aged hunter and reader suddenly decides to become a knight-errant, like the ones in the books he reads, especially the eponymous hero of the very popular fourteenth-century romance *Amadis of Gaul*, and he invents a new name for himself, Don Quixote.

> In short, his understanding being quite *perverted*, he was *seized* by the strangest whim that ever entered the brain of a *madman*. This was no other than a *persuasion*, that it was highly expedient and necessary, not only for his own honour, but also for the good of the public, that he should profess knight-errantry.... This poor *lunatic* looked upon himself already as good as seated, by his own single valour, on the throne of Trebisond; and *intoxicated* with these agreeable *vapours* of his *unaccountable folly*, resolved to put his design in practice forthwith. (1,1)

A knight-errant needs a lover, an admiring woman to whom he can dedicate his good deeds. Don Quixote just happens to pick Aldonza Lorenzo who instantly transforms from the "hale, buxom wench" he can't talk to into a transcendently beautiful princess (new name, Dulcinea del Toboso) who will instantly fall in with all his adventurous plans. She remains a chaste, Platonic lover, but they now can talk, one assumes, provided Quixote ever actually gets around to meeting her in the flesh.

It's crucial to note here that Quixote's sense of Dulcinea and knight-errantry is not completely credulous. Here and there in the novel Cervantes inserts text that indicates clearly that Quixote is aware that he has imagined Dulcinea and believes in her just the same. Herein lies an important point of psychology (within the novel) and composition: Quixote wills himself to believe in Dulcinea, knight-errantry and enchanters but must battle doubt in his own heart. He is literally of two minds. In many passages he knows and doesn't know the truth at the same moment, moments of immense complexity and internal tension.

> "...now, I remember, Dulcinea can neither read nor write, nor ever set eyes on any writing or letter of mine; for, our mutual love has been altogether platonic, without extending farther than a modest glance; and even that so seldom, that I can safely swear, in twelve years, during which I have loved her more than the light of these eyes, which will one day be closed in dust, I have not seen her more than four times, and even in these four times, perhaps, she has not perceived me looking at her more than once. Such is the restraint and reserve, in which her father Lorenzo Corchuelo, and her mother Aldonza Nogales, have brought her up! ...let it suffice, that I imagine and believe the worthy Aldonza Lorenzo, to be beautiful and modest...and these two is Dulcinea in consummate possession of.... And to conclude, I imagine that all I have said is true without exaggeration or diminution. I paint her in my fancy, according to my wish, as well in beauty as in rank...and let people say what they will, if I am blamed by the ignorant, I shall be acquitted by the most rigid of those who are proper judges of the case." (1,25)

Actually, here are those last clauses rendered by Carlos Fuentes, who makes the case a bit clearer; he calls it "one of the most moving declarations of love ever written."

> "Thus, it is enough that I think and believe that Aldonza Lorenzo is beautiful and honest; the question of class is of no consequence.... I paint her in my imagination as I desire her...and let the world think what it wants."

One of the (unconscious) results of this tension: After becoming Don Quixote, the old man turns insomniac and is given to fits of violent rage—"rage" is an oft-repeated word in the book—usually when he senses he is being mocked. He attacks farm animals, women in carriages, priests and barbers with incredible violence, all in the name of Dulcinea del Toboso. But the compositional implication of the old don's bifurcated consciousness is even more intriguing. The fact that imagined or symbolic reality exists side-by-side and simultaneously with mundane reality gives the book an odd flickering quality (I borrow the word from Viktor Shklovsky), a lightness and airiness that resists univocal interpretation.

Leaving aside the huge number of incidents, speeches, inset stories and found manuscripts that litter the path, the essential story of the novel is not difficult to tell. After deciding to be a knight-errant and inventing Dulcinea del Toboso, Quixote sets out, spends the night at an inn where he stands vigil over his armour and is knighted by the inn keeper. But this first journey abruptly ends when Quixote attacks a column of merchants on the road. Rozinante falls; merchants and retainers beat Quixote to a pulp. A kindly peasant brings him home. While Quixote lies abed recovering, the village curate and the barber, both old friends, sort through his books and burn most of them. Then they brick over his library door and tell Quixote an enchanter did it.

When he is healthy again, Quixote sets out on a second trip, this time with a peasant neighbour, Sancho Panza, on his donkey Dapple. Quixote and Sancho travel along, having many adventures. They spend one night at a second inn where Quixote causes a ruckus. He suspects the daughter of the house is in love with him. In the night, mistaking the whore Maritornes for the daughter, he drags her into his bed in order to explain to her why he can't sleep with her. Bedlam ensues. Quixote escapes, but Sancho gets tossed in a blanket.

They journey into the Sierra Morena where Quixote decides to get in touch with Dulcinea. He writes her a letter and dispatches Sancho to deliver it. Sancho only gets back as far as the inn where he runs into the curate and the barber come to rescue Don Quixote. They concoct a cover story and disguises and head into the mountains to find him. Instead they run into Dorotea in disguise—she's a character in one of the inset stories. Dorotea agrees to help in saving Quixote and pretends to be the Princess Micomicona who has journeyed from Guinea (west coast of Africa) to summon Quixote to fight a giant in her country (she promises to give Sancho an island). Sancho tells Quixote that he has delivered his letter and that Dulcinea orders him to appear before her. Regretfully, the old don decides he must first fulfill his promise to the Princess Micomicona before he can return to Toboso.

What follows is a long sequence of interwoven stories and hoaxes at this miraculous inn of crossed destinies (where earlier Sancho was tossed in a blanket and subsequently met up with the curate and barber). Don Quixote disappears for chapters at a time while other stories get told (including three chapters during which the plotters read a found manuscript called "The Impertinent Curiosity"). In his dreams, he battles the west African giant though, in fact, he has been slashing wineskins in his sleep. Maritornes torments him, catches his hands and leaves him suspended from the inn's second floor window for a night. The police come to arrest him for letting some galley slaves free in an earlier chapter. Other visitors arrive; recognitions take place; couples reconcile and reform with appropriate partners (all those inset stories); finally, the curate and his co-conspirators trap Quixote in a cage that he believes is enchanted. Resigned, the old man is trundled home in a wagon.

The second part, Volume 2 (published in 1615, as I have said), begins a month later. Somewhat miraculously, the first part has already been published and is a popular success. Quixote and Sancho meet a young student named Sampson Carrasco who has read Volume 1. Carrasco eggs Quixote on. In part he does this because he has talked to the curate and the barber and they have hatched a plan. Fearing that Quixote will break out again anyway, they take the opportunity of the book publication to encourage his mania, planning to intercept him somewhere along the way and bring about his final disillusionment (and thus return him to mental health).

There are two things to take note of at this point. First, Volume 1 tends to replace *Amadis of Gaul* as the shadow book or mediating text for the last half of the novel. Don Quixote has to live up to himself and to his readers' expectations. And second, Quixote's friends have invented a very strange method of curing him which nonetheless reminds me of certain contemporary psychoanalytic ideas (another instance of the novel's startling prescience). For example, it sounds a bit like a comic version of Lacan's notion of traversing the fantasy which, as Slavoj Zizek writes, "means *fully identifying oneself with the fantasy*—namely, the fantasy which structures the excess that resists our immersion in daily reality...." Such identification is "the concluding moment of the psychoanalytic treatment." (*Welcome to the Desert of the Real*, 17) In a sense, Quixote's friends seem to realize that in enacting his mania, in manifesting symptoms, he is closer to an underlying reality than he was as Alonso the Good (reality as a mode of banal denial). Crucially, neither the curate nor Carrasco ever ask Quixote directly to give up his fantasy; they both enter the fantasy themselves to restrain him, as it were, from the inside.

Quixote and Sancho set out for Saragossa to compete in a knightly tournament there. But first Quixote decides they must see Dulcinea. Of course, there is no Dulcinea, though Sancho has claimed to have seen her and delivered his master's letter in Volume 1. Outside Toboso they see three village girls riding out on donkeys. In a panic Sancho tells Quixote one of them is Dulcinea with a spell on her, transformed by an enchanter into the semblance of a village wench. Most of the rest of the book is built around Quixote's desire to deliver Dulcinea from this enchantment. Shortly after leaving Toboso, Quixote and Sancho meet the Knight of the Mirrors who challenges the old don to battle. Quixote defeats him; the strange knight turns out to be Carrasco, the student (though defeated and sent home, he will return). Another significant (and puzzling) incident involves the Cave of Montesinos, a mysterious hole in the ground. Quixote descends on a rope, stays down a long while and comes back claiming to have seen Dulcinea in her transformed state. (There is some flickering language here and there as the book goes on, indicating that Quixote may be trying to perpetrate a hoax of his own.)

Soon after, Quixote meets a real-life Duke and Duchess (the empty-headed dot.com millionaires of their age; one imagines them suddenly rich with all that Aztec and Inca gold; Cervantes nails them exactly) who have read the first part of the novel and are delighted to bring the knight home and humour him. What follows is again a long sequence of hoaxes. The Duke and Duchess, knowing the truth about Dulcinea from the first volume and having been told about the three village wenches at Toboso by Sancho the blabbermouth, prime their retainers to act the parts of Merlin and Dulcinea. Dulcinea begs to be released from her enchantment. Merlin says she will be released when Sancho allows himself to be whipped 3300 times. As part of the hoax, the Duke and Duchess

22

give Sancho a town (island) to govern, and for a few chapters the book splits between Sancho's adventures as a governor (he turns out to be surprisingly wise) and Quixote's adventures at the Duke's court. Chief amongst these is his relationship with a young lady named Altisidora who pretends to be in love with him and the bespectacled duenna (parallel to Maritornes in Volume 1; this sequence of actions includes another great comic bedroom scene). And once again Quixote is in mortal fear for his chastity. Sancho voluntarily resigns his post as governor, showing himself wiser than most in his willingness to abandon the promise of power and wealth in order to stay true to his heart.

Word of the spurious *Don Quixote*, mentioned above, reaches the real Don Quixote (albeit he is not quite real himself) who changes his plans to fight at Saragossa (because the spurious book already has him going and fighting there). Quixote and Sancho head to Barcelona where, amid various other adventures, humiliations and inset stories, the old don encounters on a beach one day the Knight of the White Moon who defeats him in battle and makes him swear to return home and give up knight errantry for a period of two years. The Knight of the White Moon, of course, turns out to be none other than Sampson Carrasco, the plotting student from Quixote's own village, although Quixote never finds this out himself. Knight and squire journey homeward, Quixote still insisting that Sancho receive his 3300 lashes. The word "melancholy" begins to repeat with thudding regularity. At the entrance to his village, Quixote interprets an omen to mean that he will never see Dulcinea del Toboso. He falls ill, his sanity returns, he renounces knight errantry, and dies.

Plot and Subplot, Large Structural Considerations

In contrast to the moony, sentimental, dream-the-impossible-dream visionary of ill-read popular imagination, my new reading of the novel proffers a shy, bookish, sexually-inhibited, insomniac, self-doubting, quick-tempered, obsessive-compulsive and paranoid Don

Quixote, one who attacks and defeats a woman in a carriage defended by a man with a sword and a pillow, who attacks and inflicts grievous damage on a funeral procession, who ends up at an inn over the back of a mule, who grabs Maritornes and drags her into bed in order to explain why he can't sleep with her, who takes the self-concocted balsam of Fierabras and vomits on Sancho (after which Sancho vomits on him), who whacks Sancho every time he loses his temper, whose logic is always maddeningly self-serving, who gets run over by a herd of pigs (and then a herd of bulls), who very earnestly capers about pretending to be insane in the Sierra Morena (or Brown Mountain as Smollett likes to call it), and who sits bravely ahorse through the night of the fulling mill incident (when Sancho takes a shit—this is the very image of Bakhtinian high/low comedy).

The old don reads books of romance and the books infect his brain. Books mediate reality for him and tell him how and whom to love. Once he's decided to be a knight-errant everything else in the novel follows: his wandering in search of adventures, his belief that his main enemy is an enchanter, his reinvention of the world according to premises in books, and, most especially, his idealized love of Aldonza-Dulcinea. One wants to ask here if, in a way, he loved Aldonza and made up the whole knight-errant mania in order to work out this impossible love (why impossible? because he's a nice old codger and can't possibly have an affair with her; aside from his inhibitions, class issues obviously obtain).

Everything he does is driven by his desire, his love for and service to Dulcinea del Toboso. This is the fantasy desire suggested to him by books, but it nevertheless functions throughout as the plot-drag, the *sine qua non* of plot construction. The Quixote-Dulcinea plot goes something like this: He invents her, then goes out in search of adventure to prove his love for her. In the Sierra Morena he writes a letter to her and sends it with Sancho who never delivers it. Then Sancho invents his own meeting with Aldonza-Dulcinea, saying that she orders Don Quixote to come to see her. Quixote decides that he can't go to Toboso until he's earned the right in some heroic way. Almost at once Dorotea-Princess Micomicona enlists him as a champion, putting another obstacle in his path. Now he can't go to Dulcinea till he's finished off the giant and restored the princess to her throne.

In Volume 2, Quixote starts out heading to Toboso to find her. But Sancho invents the scheme of telling him she is one of three peasant girls on donkeys. At Sancho's prompting, Quixote decides she has been enchanted. Then the whole second part is twisted around her enchantment and his desire to get her unenchanted. In the cave of Montesinos he claims to have seen her in her enchanted form. Then in the Duke's castle he is presented with a hoax, one of the servants dressed up as the enchanted Dulcinea and a made-up Merlin who says she'll be unenchanted when Sancho gives himself 3300 whip lashes. Then we go through some chapters where part of the joke is trying to get an understandably reluctant Sancho to whip himself. When the Knight of the White Moon defeats Quixote and demands that he deny Dulcinea's beauty, the old don refuses and is ready to die. At the end of the book, as he re-enters his home village, he receives a revelation or a sign that he'll never actually see her. Then he falls ill, realizes that he has been insane, renounces knight errantry and dies.

The fact that Quixote unconsciously borrows his desire (the primary impetus for plot) from the books he reads has an interesting thematic effect; it situates the crucial conflict of the novel deep inside his own head where it is nearly inaccessible both to himself and the reader. The great question of the novel is not When will he find Dulcinea? (that's Quixote's own surface idea of how the novel is structured) but How long can his imaginary world-picture maintain itself against actual events, Sancho's folksy realism, the cunning plots of Quixote's friends, the curate and the barber, and the ridicule of any number of shepherds, mule drivers, inn keepers, courtiers and slatterns? That is, the novel subverts and decentres its own structure. The question is not whether Quixote can achieve the object of his desire; rather, the novel puts into question the nature of desire itself. Not only is it impossible for him to find Dulcinea, but Quixote does not even own his own desire. That which seems most integral to himself is secondhand, mediated by books. Hence the steady drumming of the word "melancholy" as the novel turns for home, the external symptom (along with the insomnia and temper tantrums) of Quixote's self-doubt.

The second plot, the major sublot, is the Sancho plot, which involves Sancho's desire to follow Quixote in order to win an island

(Quixote tells him this is the sort of reward all squires of knights-errant can expect). In the first part of *Don Quixote*, the closest Sancho comes to this is in the Princess Micomicona hoax. He falls for the hoax, even though he is a party to it from the beginning, and thinks he will get an island. In Volume 2, the Duke, as a facet of the larger hoax, actually gives Sancho a town to govern. But Sancho finds the toils of government difficult and disappointing and he walks away from his post after governing rather well for a brief time. So Sancho is tricked all the way through by the major hoaxes (Dorotea and the curate; the Duke and Duchess), but he is also a trickster himself (he lies about delivering the letter; he lies about the peasant girl being Dulcinea). Sancho's lies have significant force in prolonging the Quixote-Dulcinea plot. Also, he unwittingly aids in the larger hoaxes by blabbing Quixote's intimate life, trials and beliefs.

Sancho's subplot in relation to Quixote's main plot is a variant of the conventional upstairs-downstairs plot-subplot structure (e.g. Lear and Gloucester). Structurally their plots are quite similar with different outcomes, which reveal essential character differences. The great Spanish critic Salvador de Madariaga, in *Don Quixote, An Introductory Essay in Psychology*, writes: "Superficial tradition has reduced its marvellous psychological fabric to a line of simplest melody. Don Quixote, a valiant knight and idealist; Sancho, a matter-of-fact and cowardly rustic. What tradition does not see is that this design which, on a first impression, is based on contrast, resolves itself into a complicated and delicate parallel, the development of which is one of the subtle achievements of this book of genius. Sancho is, up to a point, a transposition of Don Quixote in a different key. Such cases of parallelism are seldom lacking in great works of art." Another way of looking at the relationship between Don Quixote and Sancho is to think of it as one of character grouping and gradation in the sense that E. K. Brown uses those terms in *Rhythm in the Novel*. Graded characters are characters in narrative who share, in a more or less exaggerated or more or less attenuated fashion, thematically crucial experiences, attitudes or qualities with other characters in such a way as to create structural parallels.

Critics often interpret Sancho as Don Quixote's down-to-earth alter ego, the realist to his fantasist. Madariaga does a convincing job of complicating this picture, parsing the Quixote and Sancho plots in the following way. Quixote wants to be a knight-errant and honour his lover Dulcinea; in abstract terms, he wants glory. Sancho wants an island; in abstract terms, he wants power. As the novel wears on, plot and subplot subtly criss-cross: Quixote grows ever more doubtful and melancholy, culminating in his defeat by the Knight of the White Moon and his death; Sancho grows into himself, as it were, learning to speak well by imitating his master, governing his island with wisdom, and, finally, achieving dignity by walking away from the thing he seems to have most desired.

But I am not sure this analysis illuminates the whole complexity of Cervantes' construction. First of all, Quixote does give up his desire, renouncing it on his deathbed and, like Sancho, becoming himself again, at least in the sense of returning to the self he was before he became addicted to romance novels and went crazy. At the end of the novel he becomes Alonso the Good again.

> "Good gentlemen, said he, congratulate and rejoice with me, upon my being no longer Don Quixote de la Mancha, but plain Alonso Quixano, surnamed the Good, on account of the innocence of my life and conversation. I am now an enemy to Amadis of Gaul, and the whole infinite tribe of his descendants; now, are all the profane histories of knight-errantry odious to my reflection; now, I am sensible of my own madness, and the danger into which I have been precipitated by reading such absurdities...." (2,74)

Sentimental readers (the dream-the-impossible-dream school) prefer to ignore this moment or find it a puzzle. A more telling contrast between the two characters lies in the quality of their love relationships: in brief, one is married while the other is not. Don Quixote is in love with an imaginary woman, an absence; Sancho is married to Teresa Panza, a loud, spirited, common woman, and they have a marriageable daughter named Sanchica. The one man never speaks of love; the other talks about it all the time. And their criss-crossed plots raise the question: Which of these two great friends, in his heart, knows what love is?

The short answer is: perhaps neither. Keeping in mind the spinning ironies of the novel, we must check our assumptions and preconceptions at the door. Sancho is just as available to mediated desire as Quixote is, and his mental life is a fog of banal, fractured

27

and often inappropriate folk wisdom, the Wal-Mart version of Quixote's extravagant book-learning. It's just as "borrowed" in every sense of the word as the lore of knight-errantry. And to say that the social institution of marriage as practised by Sancho is more true to what we think of as love than Quixote's romantic fancy is to reveal a bias in favour of the normal and the ideology of family values. The message of their ironic juxtaposition, their parallel plots, may be that neither discourse, neither version of reality, has any more traction than the other with what stands beyond the words. To return to Lacan's notion of traversing the fantasy, we might say, in the spirit of ironic reversal, that both Sancho and Quixote were more themselves when they were not themselves.

The next plot layer is that of the curate, the barber and, later, the student, Sampson Carrasco, who all try to cure Quixote, that is, they try to bring him home where he will calm down and be safe. They also burn his books and brick over his library. Their attitude to the chivalric romances that inspire the old don to madness is not exactly an antithesis: they condemn them as untrue and misleading yet gleefully and hypocritically preserve their favourites from the holocaust. Their preferred method of operation is to engage Quixote in the discourse of his madness, they humour him, in order to lure him home.

This is a sort of counterplot, or you can see the curate as the main resistance of the novel, Quixote's enemy or the anti-Quixote. (Though it's interesting that throughout he remains Quixote's friend; he means well. There isn't a real enemy in the novel. Cervantes is quite unlike Dickens who strews his novels with malevolent characters so that he can generate a good versus evil plot-line and who relies on sentimental coincidences to create happy endings. There are no happy endings in the world of Don Quixote.) In Volume 1, the curate and the barber eventually have to drag him home in a cage. In Volume 2, on his second attempt, the student Carrasco, as the Knight of the White Moon, defeats Quixote in battle and extracts a vow from the old don to return home and retire from knight-errantry for two years. Not only do the curate and the barber engage Quixote on the level of his madness in order to cure him, they also sometimes trick him just to see him perform.

Quixote inhabits an odd, lonely universe. This is not a book about communication. Quixote pontificates and interprets the world according to his own whims and urgencies. He never has a real conversation. His is the loneliness of the insane. And I recall how often the word "melancholy" repeats as the book comes to a close. As Quixote approaches the realization that he has been mad all along, he falls deeper and deeper into depression; and he seems to understand, when it finally dawns on him that he'll never actually see Dulcinea, that he will also never have an authentic conversation with another human being—of course, this isn't in the book in so many words.

The fourth layer of plot involves what is commonly known as the picaresque aspect of the novel, all the incidents and adventures Quixote encounters simply because he is wandering through a landscape (wandering isn't quite the right word; his wandering is motivated by his desire to search for adventure in order to do honour to his Lady Dulcinea). Some of these picaresque incidents have a certain persistence within the novel structure, coming back into the plot later on. For example, the boy Don Quixote thinks he has rescued from beating and delivered to justice in Chapter 4 of Volume 1 (this is during Quixote's very first foray into the world as a knight) shows up again at the inn of hoaxes in Chapter 31; Gines de Passamonte, the criminal Quixote mistakenly releases from galley-slavery in Chapter 22 of Volume 1 (de Passamonte is also an author, writing his memoirs), shows up in the next chapter when he steals Sancho's beloved donkey Dapple and then wanders back into the novel in Chapter 30 disguised as a gypsy. In Volume 2, he appears again as the mysterious puppet-master, Mr. Peter, with his trained ape (2,25). The galley-slave incident also results in Quixote being accosted at the inn by police with a warrant for his arrest (they let him go on the grounds that an insane man would never be convicted anyway). On this and other similar minor repetitions, Vladimir Nabokov says, "An important note of structure: Cervantes for the sake of keeping the novel together..., has the characters either recall past events or has characters from former chapters appear again...the continuation and development of these episodes along the main current do give the story the kind of sweeping unity that in our minds is associated with the form of the novel." (*Lectures on Don Quixote*, 141-142)

29

Structurally, the book splits into two parts, two volumes. They both move through a series of individual adventures toward a long segment of greater complication having to do with one group of characters tricking Quixote (Dorotea and the curate; the Duke and Duchess and, yes, the curate again and the student Sampson Carrasco). In Volume 1, all the trickery centres around that fabulous inn wherein Quixote pulls Maritornes into bed with him. In Volume 2, it takes place at the castle of the Duke and Duchess (where Altisidora pretends to be in love with him, and the bespectacled Donna Rodriguez plays the Maritornes role). The hoax is more developed in the second volume than the first. In both parts, Sancho contributes a significant lie to propel the Quixote-Dulcinea plot (and in both parts, Sancho's donkey gets stolen briefly). But in both he ends up being tricked as well though with one significant difference: near the end of the second volume, Sancho renounces his desire to govern an island.

In Volume 1, the hoaxes develop out of the inset story plots and characters, which seem oddly tacked onto the novel, whereas, in the second volume, the Duke and Duchess seem rather more organic to the whole. They are in the book because they have read the first volume. These tacked on plots (inset stories, found manuscripts, etc.) are mostly tales of love, betrayal, jealousy, disguise, recognition, etc. with somewhat generic, thinly characterized protagonists. They remind me of contemporary TV soap operas with their conventional set-ups and interchangeably gorgeous, young actors. In Volume 1, Dorotea has her own (tacked on) plot but, for the sake of diversion, falls in with the curate's plan to humour and cure Quixote. In Volume 2, many of the people Quixote meets are motivated by their role as readers of Volume 1. And even later there are people who have read the spurious second part (based on a real spurious continuation of Cervantes' novel that nonetheless seems to fit rather nicely in the novel because it extends the pattern of proliferating Quixote texts and proliferating mirrors of reality). Perhaps one of the saddest moments in the novel is the horrific chapter in which Quixote begs for a testimonial that endorses him as the true Quixote. Because he is a creature of words, the proliferation of Quixote texts corrupts and even destroys his identity. Not only does he lose Dulcinea, but he loses himself, both of which were illusory in the first place. He loses what he never had, though he did believe he had it. At the very end of the novel, he realizes that his beliefs were illusory. Sadness upon sadness.

The two large plot movements of the novel thus follow a similar repeating pattern: love, journey, hoax, defeat, return. There is actually a third repetition of this plot, only in the fainter key, right at the beginning. Quixote's first sortie, without Sancho, takes just a couple of days or so. And there is no hoax (unless you count the innkeeper going along with the vigil idea). So: love, journey, minor hoax, defeat, return. This works as an overture to the whole, though Nabokov suggests that this short first journey was meant as a short story, which Cervantes then expanded as its possibilities became clearer to him (*Lectures on Don Quixote*, 28).

Note: Nabokov's *Don Quixote* is a head-scratcher; he can't quite bring himself to warm to it. After demolishing most of the standard critics who have barely read the novel, as far as he's concerned, he gets into a puzzle over how such a chaotic, technically primitive and cruel book could become so famous. He suggests that somehow the idea of the novel, sentimentalized and idealized, has come detached from the actual novel. And certainly that's true to an extent. But Nabokov seems to have a blind spot, doesn't want to see how patterned and organized the book actually is, doesn't want to admit even what his own reading tells him. Any evidence of planning and pattern strikes Nabokov as astonishing. He spends a good deal of one lecture going through each conflict Quixote encounters, totting up the wins and losses.

> In terms of encounters, the score is even: twenty victories against twenty defeats. Moreover, in each of the two parts of the book the score is also even: 13 to 13 and 7 to 7, respectively. This perfect balance of victory and defeat is very amazing in what seems such a disjoined and haphazard book. It is due to a secret sense of writing, the harmonizing intuition of the artist. (*Lectures on Don Quixote*, 110)

Nabokov's reluctance, in that last sentence, to accord Cervantes any self-conscious compositional talent is nothing short of hilarious in that it completely contradicts everything he has so arduously discovered in the previous twenty pages of analysis. (Despite his blind spots and hobbyhorses, Nabokov remains a great reader—counting up the number of victories and defeats was a brilliant idea.)

The Labyrinth of Mirrors

In interpreting the world, Quixote tends to see ordinary things as if they were projections of what he reads in books. For example, two flocks of sheep become two armies of knights. An inn becomes a castle. But then occasionally he will surprise the reader (and Sancho) by seeing something as it really is. When the three peasant girls come riding out of Toboso on donkeys, to Quixote they look like three peasant girls on donkeys. So there is a kind of running joke here; the reader begins to expect Quixote to act one way and then gets a pleasant comic surprise when he doesn't. But the thread that runs through all these events is Quixote's notion that he is bedeviled by some envious enchanter (Freston is the first one mentioned by name) who transforms things in order to confuse and defeat him. When he attacks the windmills: 1) he transforms the windmills into giants in his mind, 2) after crashing into the windmill, he decides that a wicked enchanter has disguised the giants as windmills to mock him. That is, the modus operandi is a three-step dance. First of all, Quixote sometimes sees the world as it really is. But other times he sees the world as from inside a book, through the grid of his obsession. And when forced to acknowledge some reality or when he's defeated, he falls back on the enchanter logic to explain the apparent anomaly. In the encounter with the three peasant girls riding out of Toboso, Sancho tries to work the obsession logic, hoping Quixote will simply see the peasant girl as Dulcinea. But when that doesn't work, Sancho falls back on the enchanter argument to convince Quixote that this is Dulcinea. So we get the scene in which Quixote falls to his knees before a woman he sees as a peasant girl but who he believes is Dulcinea transformed.

Add to this the complication of the cave of Montesinos episode and certain knowing things that Quixote says about his "belief" in Dulcinea ("God knows whether or not there is such a person as Dulcinea in the world, whether she is fantastical or not fantastical; for, these things are not to be too nicely investigated...." (2,32)). These elements introduce a thread of self-consciousness in Quixote which seriously challenges any simple conjecture about the meaning of his madness and his book. Or it deepens his character. There is an implication that his madness is partly put on, that his consciousness flickers; one pulls back from saying he struggles with himself, though the cave of Montesinos episode and the affair of Clavelino, the flying horse, interject a fascinating element of self-questioning or self-uneasiness or even reverse hoaxing.

At the cave of Montesinos, Quixote has himself lowered into the grotto on a rope and is pulled up an hour later, claiming he has been underground three days dreaming of long-dead French knights, Merlin and Dulcinea, who sends her maid to borrow money from him. Sancho, with unusual bluntness, accuses him of lying for he knows the truth about Dulcinea. In an aside, the narrative indicates that, on his deathbed, Quixote confessed to making the whole story up. (2,22) Later in the novel, Quixote seems confused, wondering himself whether he really saw Dulcinea or only dreamed her. One of the hoaxes invented by the Duke and Duchess is to supply Quixote and Sancho with a mechanical flying horse called Clavelino on which they can fly to the stars. What ensues is a truly pathetic scene: old don and squire blindfolded on something like a child's rocking horse, surrounded by smirking courtiers. Sancho and Quixote seem to be fooled, seem to think they are zooming among the constellations. Sancho claims he covertly lifted his blindfold and saw the stars whizzing by. But Don Quixote sidles up to Sancho and whispers, "Heark ye, Sancho; since you would have us believe what you say, touching the things you saw in heaven, I desire the like credit from you, with regard to those things I saw in the cave of Montesinos. That's all." (2,41)

The book thus develops a rather complicated layering of reality-discourses: 1) the common-or-garden variety reality (windmills), 2) Quixote's out-of-a-book reinterpretation of reality (giants), 3) either world transformed into the other by an enchanter (giants into windmills, Dulcinea into a peasant girl on a donkey). To this Cervantes adds the element of hoaxing (and reverse hoaxing) that runs through the book, as soon as people begin to read Quixote's modus operandi. People play tricks on Quixote for two basic reasons: 1) to humour him (so as to be able to get through a scrape, avoid his temper, or cure him), and 2) to entertain themselves. Often they are doing both at the same time. Cervantes seems to want us to think that the curate and barber and the Duke and Duchess have a lot of affection for the old codger even as they laugh at him (it was a more adolescent time).

Cervantes makes considerable use of what I call point-of-view cascades like the following small extract from the episode of the attack on the funeral procession. Note the point-of-view sequence: external observer, the mourners, Sancho and Don Quixote.

> The mourners being involved and entangled in their long robes, could not stir out of the way: so Don Quixote, without running any risk, drubbed them all round, and obliged them at length to quit the field, much against their inclination; for, they actually believed that he was no man, but a devil incarnate, who lay in wait to carry off the dead body that was in the litter.
>
> All this while Sancho stood beholding with admiration the courage and intrepidity of the knight; saying within himself: "This master of mine is certainly as strong and valiant as he pretends to be."
>
> Meanwhile, Don Quixote, by the light of a torch that lay burning on the ground, perceiving the first whom the mule had overthrown, rode up to him, and clapping the point of his lance to the poor man's throat, commanded him to yield.... (1,19)

Sometimes Cervantes piles the point-of-view layers on so thickly that the scenes spiral into a vertiginous whirl of realities or meanings. This happens when he combines the two Quixote realities with a hoax and adds his cunning use of third-person multiple point of view (which functions magically throughout). So you find scenes in which a hoaxer will be humouring Quixote and some other person, who is not in on the joke and also not in on Quixote's modus operandi, will get angry and frustrated. And in a sadder version of this, there are scenes in which Quixote vainly asks for someone outside the situation to tell him what is real.

The following is a long passage—a more complicated version of a point-of-view cascade—that gives the flavour of the whole. The scene takes place at the aforementioned inn of crossed destinies in the first part of *Don Quixote*. Earlier, the old don attacked a barber on the road and stole his brass basin, which he believed to be the famous helmet of Mambrino. As an afterthought, Sancho took some of the barber's donkey harness (pannel) as spoils of victory. Now the barber arrives at the inn, recognizes his harness, and asks for it and

34

his basin back. The point-of-view layers include the barber claiming theft, the barber from Don Quixote's own village pretending to believe the old don, the curate and several characters from the inset stories, a confused Don Quixote, some servants and four members of the Holy Brotherhood (the police).

"[Italics added for emphasis.] Gentlemen, said *the barber*, pray, favour me with your opinion, concerning what is affirm'd by these gentlefolks, who so obstinately maintain that this is not a bason but a helmet?" "And if anyone affirms to the contrary, replied *Don Quixote*, I will make him sensible that he lies, if he be a knight; and if a plebeian, that he lies a thousand times." *His own townsman* [Don Quixote's friend, the barber from his own village], who was present all the while, being well-acquainted with the knight's humour, resolved to encourage him in his extravagance, and carry on the joke for the diversion of the company: with this view, he addressed himself to the other shaver, saying, "Mr. Barber, or whosoever you are, you must know that I am of the same profession: I have had a certificate of my examination these twenty years; and I know very well, all the instruments of the art, without excepting one: I was moreover a soldier in my youth, consequently can distinguish an helmet, a morrion, and a casque, with its beaver, together with everything relating to military affairs; I mean, the different kinds of armour wore by soldiers in the field: I say, under correction, and still with submission to better judgment, that the object now in dispute, which that worthy gentleman holds in his hand, is not only no barber's bason, but also, as far from being one as black is from white, or falsehood from truth. I likewise aver that tho' it is an helmet, it is not entire." "You are certainly in the right, said Don Quixote, for it wants one half, which is the beaver."

The curate, who by this time, understood the intention of his friend, seconded this asseveration which was also confirmed by Cardenio, Don Fernando, and his companions, and *the judge himself* would have bore a part in the jest, had he not been engrossed by the affair of Don Lewis....

35

"Good God! cried *the barber*, with amazement, is it possible that so many honourable persons should pronounce this bason to be a helmet! an assertion sufficient to astonish the whole university.... Well, if that bason be a helmet, I suppose the pannel must be a horse's trappings too, as this gentleman says." "To me it seems a pannel, replied *the knight*: but, as I have observed, I will not pretend to decide whether it be the pannel of an ass, or the furniture of a steed." "Don Quixote has no more to do but speak his opinion, said *the curate*; for, in affairs of chivalry, all these gentlemen, and even the ladies, yield to his superior understanding." "By heaven! gentlemen, cried *the knight*, do many strange accidents have happened to me, twice that I have lodged in this castle, that I will not venture positively to affirm the truth of anything that may be relating to it; for, I imagine that every thing in this place is conducted by the power of enchantment.... For me therefore, to give my opinion in a case of such perplexity, would be a rash decision: with regard to the helmet which they say is a bason, I have already expressed my sentiments; but, dare not give a definitive sentence, by declaring, whether that be a pannel, or horse's furniture. That I leave to the judgment of the good company; who, not being knights as I am, perhaps are not subjected to the inchantments of this place, but, enjoying their faculties clear and undisturbed, can judge of these things, as they really and truly are, not as they appear to my imagination." "Doubtless, replied *Don Fernando*, signor Don Quixote manifests his own prudence, in observing, that to us belongs the determination of this affair, which, that it may be the better founded, I will, in private, take the opinions of this company, one by one, and then openly declare the full result of my inquiry."

To those who were acquainted with the knight's humour, this proposal afforded matter of infinite diversion; but, the rest being ignorant of the joke, looked upon it as a piece of downright madness: this was particularly the opinion of *the domestics belonging to Don Lewis, which was even espoused by himself and four travellers just arrived*, who seemed to be troopers of the holy brotherhood, as indeed they were; but, he that almost ran distracted, was *the barber whose bason was*, even in his own sight, transformed into Mambrino's helmet.... "May I never taste the joys of heaven! cried the transported barber, if you are not all deceived; and so may my soul appear before God, as this appears to me, a meer pannel, and not the furniture of an horse! but thus might overcomes—I say no more, neither am I drunk, being fresh and fasting from everything but sin."

The company laughed as heartily at the simplicity of the barber as the extravagance of the knight.... *One of the four servants belonging to Don Lewis* now interposed, saying, "If this be not a premeditated joke, I cannot persuade myself that people of sound understanding...should venture to say and affirm, that this is no bason, nor that a pannel; yet, seeing this is both said and affirmed, I conceive there must be some mystery in thus insisting upon a thing so contrary to truth and experience; for, by God! (an oath he swore with great emphasis) all the people on earth shall never make me believe that this is not a barber's bason, or that not the pannel of an he-ass."....

At the same time, *one of the troopers*, who had entered and been witness to the quarrel and question, could no longer contain his choler and displeasure at what he heard, and therefore said, in a furious tone, "If that is not a pannel, my father never begat me; and he that says, or shall say the contrary, must be drunk." "You lie, like an infamous scoundrel, replied *Don Quixote*, who lifting up his lance, which he still kept in his hand, aimed such a stroke at the trooper's skull, that if he had not been very expeditious in shifting it, he would have been stretched at full length upon the ground.... (1,45)

Yet another level of reality discourse develops late in the novel when Quixote meets people who have read the spurious second part and we get the odd situation of a character in a work of fiction fighting for his own sense of his reality. This extends the epistemological helplessness Quixote endures in the scene just quoted, the helplessness of a thinking subject in the relativistic universe of a novel. (How modern this novel sounds sometimes: a subject trying

37

to swim in a whirlpool of relative truths; a knight, as Quixote writes to Dulcinea, "wounded by the edge of absence." (1,25)) The saddest moment in this sequence comes when the old don, confused, shocked and exhausted, asks someone (who has read the spurious second part and claims to have actually met a knight known as Don Quixote) to sign a testimonial to the effect that he is the real article. "...the deposition was drawn up in the strongest terms, and the knight and the squire were as much rejoiced, as if this certificate had been of the utmost consequence to their destiny...." (2,72)

The effect here is analogous to the one Tolstoy achieves in respect to character in *War and Peace*. As Henri Troyat, Tolstoy's biographer, writes (note that the example he cites is a version of the point-of-view cascade):

> What gives so much life to the protagonists in *War and Peace* is that they are all defined in terms of one another. E.g. "Returning to Moscow from the army, Nicholas Rostov was welcomed *by his close relatives* as the best of sons, a hero, the irreplaceable Nikolenka; *by the other members of his family* as a pleasant easy-going and well-mannered young man; *by his friends* as a good-looking lieutenant of hussars, a first-rate dancer and one of the most eligible young men in Moscow." Through a thousand observations of this type Tolstoy creates a definite atmosphere around each of his characters. Each one is caught up in an extremely subtle net of sympathies and antipathies. His slightest gesture resounds in several other consciousnesses. Prince Andrey, Pierre, Natasha, and Princess Marya are not flat images, always seen from the same side; the reader moves around them and feels their interdependence with all the other characters. They all obey the law of relativity.

According to Troyat, after rewriting a scene four times so that it would be impossible to tell which side he favoured, Tolstoy wrote: "I have found that a story leaves a deeper impression when it is impossible to tell which side the author is on."

But whereas in Tolstoy's novel the point-of-view cascade enhances verisimilitude by creating a sense of character in the round, as it were, in Cervantes' novel these structures—Don Quixote's mental modus operandi, the various reality-discourses, the hoaxes, and the cascading points of view—combine to create the novel as a complex relativity machine, an immense shimmering surface, a labyrinth of mirrors, in which nothing is what it seems, only what it seems to a particular character at a particular time. Truth slips along the sentences like a will o' the wisp. Or it is built up by superimposing overlapping images, none of which, in itself, is truth. Truth is in a sentence's relation to another sentence *within the novel*, less a matter of reference to external reality than of a mysterious vibratory coherence.

The reader, privy to all points of view, seems to stand with the author outside the novel and see clearly what the characters only see from an angle. This is one of the strange beauties of the novel, the aesthetic flickering (again, that word) between inside and outside. It creates a pleasant sense of certainty amidst uncertainty, a playfulness, a lightness—which, in the end, is beguiling and possibly deceptive. For by the close of the novel Cervantes has pricked the balloon of reader certainty over and over again. For example, the reader never knows what actually happened in the cave of Montesinos, and, later, the Don Quixote impostor, who enters the novel as a fictional character in the spurious second volume, erupts into *Don Quixote* itself as a real if debased double of the old knight himself. The latter is an instance of the bookish games Cervantes plays with the logic of reality, text and fiction. In other passages, he discusses the composition of the book, talks about its critical reception, and otherwise tries to seduce the reader into the relativized universe of his characters just as his characters become readers.

This reader abuse is quite clearly meant as an antidote to the kind of lazy, simple-minded reading that drives Alonso Quixano insane. Novels that present themselves as illusions, as substitute realities, are false; only books that advertise their bookish nature, that foreground their technological role in the production of illusion, are true.

Chinese Boxes and Russian Dolls, or
How the Magician Seems to Disappear
into the Hat with the Rabbit

These various structures, which can all be subsumed under the idea of point of view, seem awfully complicated though they remain systematic and finite. But Cervantes, who sometimes seems positively obsessed with distancing himself, as author, from anything written in the book (and the truth thereof), invents yet another set of textual interfaces based on a series of nested narrators (or Chinese box narrators, as Mario Vargas Llosa calls them) which fit inside one another like those Matrioshka dolls you buy in Russian souvenir shops.

1) There is an authorial first-person narrator who is ultimately responsible for the whole book and who seems to be someone like Miguel de Cervantes but who lets the reader know in the opening sentence of the novel that he will never be completely forthcoming or trustworthy. "In a certain corner of La Mancha, the name of which I do not choose to remember, there lately lived one of those country gentlemen...." (1,1) On the second page of the novel, the authorial first-person narrator mentions other authors who have written about the old knight, authors whom he has apparently consulted in researching the book we are reading. A bit later in the chapter he refers to them as "authors of this authentic history." In the second chapter, he records disagreement among these authors (there seem to be a lot of them).

> Some authors say his first adventure was that of the pass
> of Lapice, but others affirm, that the windmills had the
> maidenhead of his valour: all that I can aver of the matter,
> in consequence of what I found recorded in the annals of la
> Mancha, is, that having travelled the whole day.... (1,2)

Then, abruptly, at the end of Chapter 8, in the midst of Quixote's battle with the Biscayan, these primary authors break off.

> ...but the misfortune is, that in this very critical instant,
> the author of this history has left this battle in suspense,

excusing himself; that he could find no other account of Don Quixote's exploits, but what has already been related. True it is that the second author of this work, could not believe that such a curious history was consigned to oblivion; nor, that there could be such a scarcity of curious virtuosi in la Mancha, but that some papers relating to this famous knight should be found in their archives or cabinets: and therefore, possessed of this opinion, he did not despair of finding the conclusion of this delightful history, which indeed he very providentially lighted upon, in the manner which will be related.... (1,8)

This is a bit confusing because now we have a first author and a second author, both, I assume, among the authors mentioned above (or perhaps the "second author" is the first-person narrator speaking of himself in the magisterial third person). Nevertheless, the authorial first-person narrator regains the reins of the narrative on the next page, expressing his surprise and disappointment at the sudden loss of story. Then, miraculously, he stumbles upon the rest of the book.

2) While walking in the market in Toledo, the authorial first-person narrator is accosted by a boy hawking old papers. Some of them are in Arabic, so he casts about for a "Portuguese moor" to translate for him. This translator becomes the next filter between us and the story and between Cervantes and the story, the next box inside the box of narrators.

In short, I lighted upon one, to whom expressing my desire, and putting the pamphlet into his hands, he opened it in the middle, and after having read a few lines, began to laugh; when I asked the cause of his laughter, he said it was occasioned by a whimsical annotation in the margin of the book: I begged he would tell me what it was, and he answered, still laughing. What I find written on the margin, is to this purpose: "The same Dulcinea so often mentioned in the history, is said to have had the best hand at salting pork of any woman in la Mancha." (1,9)

The title of this work, it turns out, is "The History of Don Quixote

de la Mancha, written by Cid Hamet Benengeli, an Arab author."
The authorial first-person narrator buys the papers and quickly
retires to the cloisters of the cathedral with his Portuguese Moor
translator to have the pages read to him. This translator is not
particularly important as an interface, though he appears several
times in the novel, once, for example, to suggest that a passage of
Sancho's dialogue is apocryphal because it's too high flown and
educated (2,5) and again to indicate that he has left out some
lengthy descriptions as being an unwarranted digression (2,18).

3) This Arabic manuscript, astonishingly enough, turns out to be
the main source for most of the novel. I say astonishing because the
implied message loop is incredibly complex both historically and
sociologically. The Moors, North-African Arabs, invaded Europe
through Spain in 711 A.D. at the tail-end of the Dark Ages and
were only stopped from colonizing France by Charlemagne at the
Battle of Tours in 732 (hence Napoleon's dictum, "Africa begins at
the Pyrenees"). The Christian kings and knights of Castile struggled
with the Moors for 781 years (the Matter of Spain, the epic poem
The Cid, belongs to this period), until, in 1492, in a spasm of ethnic
cleansing, the last Moors were expelled from Spain (along with the
Jews and Gypsies). In a sense, the Spanish Inquisition functioned as
an ongoing instrument of this policy of cultural purification,
rooting out, along with Christian heretics, converted Moors and
Jews who tried to stay behind after the retreat of the Moslem
caliphates. The Battle of Lepanto at which Cervantes himself was
wounded and captured was simply a continuation of these wars of
expulsion between Christian and Moslem (just as they continue to
this day in Bosnia and Kosovo). The Moor is the original dark other
of European consciousness.
    In the character of Cid Hamet Benengeli ("Beans-and-Jelly" as
Sancho calls him) Cervantes has chosen to have his historic cultural
and racial enemy, the epitome of what is not white, not European,
not Christian, tell the story of the new cultural hero. It makes the
story of the story even more strange and twisty; it does what Viktor
Shklovsky says art should do: delay, deform, frame and bracket the
story so as to make it seem unusual and even foreign. And it is also
an image of Cervantes' humane generosity; his dark other, in the
image of Cid Hamet Benengeli, becomes his dark brother and co-

author. But right away, of course, the truth of the story becomes suspect.

> ...if any objection can be started to the truth of this, it can be no other, but that the author was an Arabian, of a nation but too much addicted to falsehood, tho' as they are at present our enemies, it may be supposed, that he has rather failed than exceeded in the representation of our hero's exploits: for, in my opinion, when he had frequently opportunities, and calls to exercise his pen in the praise of such an illustrious knight, he seems to be industriously silent on the subject...and, if any thing seems imperfect, I affirm it must be owing to the fault of the infidel its author.... (1,9)

At the beginning of Volume 2, when Don Quixote himself hears about the publication of Volume 1, he expresses almost exactly identical suspicions.

> ...but he became uneasy again, when he recollected that his author was a Moor, as appeared by the name of Cid, and that no truth was to be expected from that people, who are all false, deceitful, and chimerical. He was afraid that his amours were treated with some indecency.... (2,3)

The authorial first-person narrator does come to trust his Arab chronicler and eventually throws aside his knee-jerk cultural attitudes, in part because Benengeli seems to have lived in la Mancha and known some of the participants in the story. He becomes the "sage Benengeli," "the Arabian and Manchegan author." (1,12) And the authorial first-person narrator says, "...be this as it will, Cid Hamet Benengeli was a most curious historian, and punctual to admiration...." (1,16) But there is considerable byplay throughout the novel involving Benengeli who remains a shadowing presence in almost every chapter. One sort of byplay is cultural, and in Volume 2 there is a curiously comic pair of parallel passages involving minor sworn oaths.

> "Blessed be the almighty Ala!" saith Cid Hamet Benengeli, in the beginning of this chapter; and this benediction he repeats three times, in consequence of finding Don Quixote and Sancho in the field again (2,8)

Cid Hamet, author of this sublime history, begins this chapter with these words; "I swear, as a catholic christian:" and upon that occasion, the translator observes, that Cid Hamet being a Moor, as he certainly was, in swearing as a catholic christian means no more than that, as a catholic christian, when he makes oath, swears he will speak the truth, and nothing but the truth, in like manner he would adhere to it.... (2,27)

(It's interesting to note in these passages that clearly the text we have is not written by Benengeli but by the authorial first-person narrator who is mostly using the Benengeli text but sometimes jumps in and out of it as does that Portuguese moorish translator— that flickering quality again.)

Benengeli also enters the text as commentator and critic in passages like the following, which comes just after that puzzling cave of Montesinos episode in which Don Quixote himself might be playing a hoax. These marginal comments add yet another category of text to the novel, which, at this juncture, is clearly taking on all the attributes of a postmodern metafictional construct.

He who translated this sublime history from the original, composed by its author Cid Hamet Benengeli, says, that turning to the chapter which treats of the adventure of the cave, he found this observation written on the margin, in the hand-writing of the said Hamet.

"I cannot conceive or persuade myself that the valiant Don Quixote literally saw and heard all that is recounted in the foregoing chapter, for this reason.... Reader, if thou hast discernment, thou mayest judge for thyself; for it is neither my duty, nor is it in my power, to do more: tho' it is held for certain, that the knight, on his death-bed, retracted the whole, saying he had invented the story because it seemed to agree and quadrate with those adventures he had read in his books." (2,24)

This is a crucial piece of information, delivered as an aside in a text within a text. It signals Quixote's crumbling faith in his own chivalric agenda and his pathetically childish lie in the face of countervailing reality. On the scale of sadness, this is one of the most beleaguered moments in the novel; and yet it is so oddly written in. Again we need to try to make mental maps of the intricate message loops Cervantes is constructing here, the pulsing, whirling life of the text, like the spinning of sub-atomic particles.

4) At a certain point, *Don Quixote* seems so structurally complicated that one begins to lose a clear sense of how the devices should be described. In discussing the third-person multiple point-of-view strategy, I came up with the idea of a point-of-view cascade. The Chinese box narrators are technically outside this point-of-view structure, but they layer the narrative itself with a superstructure of points of view. And besides the third-person multiple structure and the Chinese box narrators, there are yet other narrative devices that interrupt, comment on, contribute to, ironize and otherwise skew or interfere with (for want of a better phrase) the story of Don Quixote. I am thinking here of the malign or merely careless typographer, the picky readers and the literary critics mentioned in Volume 2.

Cervantes invents the device of the careless typographer because of his own carelessness and haste in composing his novel (it's probably too much of a stretch to suggest that he intended the mistakes as a joke from the start, but you never know). There are several more or less important blunders in the first part of the novel that quickly became apparent to critics when the book was published in 1605. Chief amongst these is the miraculous reappearance of Sancho's beloved donkey Dapple, which is stolen by the escaped galley slave Gines de Passamonte while Sancho sleeps in Chapter 23 of Volume 1. Yet about twenty lines later we find Sancho "sitting sideways on his ass." In Chapter 25 he is once again complaining about the fact that Dapple was stolen and begging the use of Rozinante "to supply the want of Dapple: by which means a great deal of time will be saved in my going and coming." In Volume 2, Chapter 3, the student Sampson Carrasco tells Don Quixote and Sancho "the number of those who are delighted with your history, is infinite; tho' some accuse the author's memory as false or faulty." In the following chapter, Sancho tries to explain the circumstances of Dapple's theft and the old don supplies an apt literary allusion to support the explanation. But the explanation doesn't clear up the miracle of the reappearing donkey; hence the invention of the careless typesetter.

45

"The error lies not in that part of the history, replied the batchelor, but, consists in the author's saying that Sancho rode on the same ass, before it appears, that he had retrieved it." "As to that affair, said the squire, I can give you no satisfactory answer, perhaps, it was an oversight in the historian, or owing to the carelessness of the printer." (2,4)

Then, since Cervantes seems intent on mocking everything including his own mistakes, the whole issue repeats with the reappearance of Gines de Passamonte, the original donkey thief.

This Gines de Passamonte, whom Don Quixote called Ginesillo de Parapilla, was the very thief who stole Sancho's Dapple, and as, through the fault of the printers, neither the time nor the manner of the conveyance is described, in the first part of the book, many people ascribed this error of the press to want of memory in the author.... (2,27)

What is truly remarkable, playful and liberating in these passages is the interplay between the author/narrator, real readers and critics of the text and invented mischievous printers corrupting the text. It is the novelistic equivalent of breaking through the fourth wall and incorporating the audience into the text, even in a sense recreating the audience as a co-author. It draws attention to the book as a book by letting the reader in on the secrets of composition. It attacks the notion of suspension of disbelief. It subverts the "illusion" of verisimilitude. And it posits the counter-intuitive notion that a book that is against books is true.

This interplay between audience, author and text can be seen functioning at the structural level as well. It's clear that the second part of the novel is in many ways better composed in a structural sense than the first part (at the same time it shows other signs of being more hastily written). In the first part of *Don Quixote* the main Quixote-Dulcinea plot is constantly being interrupted or shunted aside to accommodate the large number of inset stories. Eventually, Cervantes warps the inset stories (via Dorotea's enlistment in the main plot action) into some sort of relationship (aside from Dorotea, the relationship is mostly geographical—everything takes place in that inn) with the main plot. This weakness didn't escape the early critics and it clearly rankled Cervantes who worked off his vexation in the usual manner by putting the objection into the novel and letting his characters deal with it humourously.

> "One of the faults that are found in the history, added the batchelor, is, that the author has inserted in it, a novel intitled The Impertinent Curiosity? Not that the thing in itself is bad, or poorly executed; but, because it is unreasonable, and has nothing to do with the story of his worship signor Don Quixote." "I'll lay a wager, cried Sancho, that this son of a cur has made a strange hodge-podge of the whole." "Now, I find, said the knight, that the author of my history is no sage, but some ignorant prater, who, without either judgment or premeditation, has undertaken to write it at random, like Orbaneja the painter of Ubeda, who being asked what he painted, answered, "Just as it happens;" (2,3)

As it happens, this is one of the criticisms levelled against the book by some modern commentators. And it's fascinating to conjecture that Cervantes did listen to his early readers; for, though there are still inset stories in Volume 2, they don't intrude to the same degree on the development of the main plot. Where Dorotea is parachuted into the main plot as a diversion from her own pressing issues (to which she returns when she isn't conning Don Quixote), the Duke and Duchess function only on the main plot. Also they are motivated by having read Volume 1 in just the way Quixote himself is prompted to renew his adventures upon hearing that he is the hero of a published book. There is a much stronger sense of organic development and unity in the second half of the novel than in the first. In any event, in one of those strange, convoluted message loops (Cervantes writing the authorial first-person narrator writing the Portuguese Moor translator rewriting Cid Hamet Benengeli), this is exactly what the novel (let me restrain myself from saying Cervantes) tells us has happened.

> The original of the history, it is said, relates that the interpreter did not translate this chapter as it had been written by Cid Hamet Benengeli, who bewails his fate in having undertaken such a dry and confined history as that

of Don Quixote; which obliged him to treat of nothing but the knight and his squire, without daring to launch out into other more grave and entertaining episodes, and digressions. He complained, that to be thus restricted in his hand, his pen, and his invention, to one subject only, so as to be obliged to speak through the mouths of a few persons, was an insupportable toil, that produced no fruit to the advantage of the author; and that, in order to avoid the inconvenience, he had in the first part used the artifice of some novels, such as the Impertinent Curiosity, and the Captive, which were detached from the history, although many particulars there recounted are really incidents which happened to Don Quixote; and, therefore, could not be suppressed. It was likewise his opinion, as he observes, that many readers being wholly ingrossed with the exploits of Don Quixote, would not bestow attention upon novels, but pass them over either with negligence or disgust, without adverting to the spirit or artifice they contain; a truth which would plainly appear, were they to be published by themselves, independent of the madness of Don Quixote, and the simplicities of Sancho. He would not therefore insert in the second part any novels, whether detached or attached; but only a few episodes that seem to spring from those very incidents which truth presents; and, even these, as brief and concise as they could possibly be related: and since he includes and confines himself within the narrow limits of narration, tho' his abilities and understanding are sufficient to treat of the whole universe, he hopes that his work will not be depreciated, and begs he may receive due praise, not for what he has written, but for what he has left unwrit. (2,44)

The sublime comedy of these verbal contortions explodes in that last clause, the grumpy Cid Hamet Benengeli begging praise for the stories he left out of the novel because he left them out of the novel. But then you think again and go back to the first lines and realize that what you have just read—Cid Hamet Benengeli's complaints and compositional rationales—are words that technically shouldn't actually be there on the page; these are the words of the chapter that the translator chose not to translate—a stunning virtuoso piece of verbal prestidigitation, Cervantes writing and unwriting the words as he goes, so that the syntax implodes and erases itself. Sometimes it seems mysterious to me that certain modern literary theorists have not seen fit to crown Cervantes as the inventor and master of almost every possible textual relationship between author, reader, text, silence (not-text), narrator and character.

5) But that's not all. There remains the curious spurious *Don Quixote*, the real fake sequel by the anonymous Tordesillan author whose name we will never know. This is another fascinating gambit by Cervantes, an author who seems willing to throw everything that comes his way into his book and make it work, also the last permutation of actual, marginal, translated, repressed or virtual texts within texts. Significantly, Don Quixote himself never gets to read any of the first part (though the reader does); he just hears about it. But he does read a few pages of the spurious second part (and the reader doesn't).

> Which he took from his companion and put in the hand of Don Quixote, who, without answering one word, began to turn over the leaves, and in a very little time gave it back to the stranger, saying, "In the little I have read, I find three things worthy of reprehension in the author; first, some expressions in the prologue or preface; secondly, his using the Aragonian dialect, and writing sometimes without articles; and, thirdly, that which confirms my opinion of his ignorance, his erring and deviating from the truth in the most material circumstance of the history; for, he says the wife of my squire Sancho Panza, is called Mary Gutierrez, whereas her name is Teresa Panza: now, if he blunders in such an essential circumstance, we may justly conclude that his whole history is full of mistakes." (2,59)

The trick (joke) here is that, in fact, the Mary Gutierrez/Teresa Panza blunder is a mistake Cervantes himself made in the real *Don Quixote*. In Volume 1, Chapter 4, Cervantes refers to Sancho's wife as Juana Gutierrez and then, four lines later, as Mary Gutierrez. She doesn't become Teresa Panza until Chapter 52. The message loop works something like this: in the novel, Don Quixote leafs through the pages of the real spurious continuation of his adventures, but, when he speaks, he speaks in the voice of a critic of the real first part of *Don Quixote*, the sort of nit-picky small-minded critics who swoop down on tiny slips to undermine the whole work. One assumes Cervantes had to deal with such critics (they're still around), and this is his sarcastic rejoinder. But what is fascinating is the number of verbal constructs he is asking the reader to hold in mind simultaneously.

A little later, in Volume 2, Chapter 62, during his visit to Barcelona, the old don takes time to explore a printing shop only to discover a proofreader working over a copy of the spurious book. (In how many novels has the hero journeyed with such intrepidity to the source of his very being? Cervantes' metafictional glee is only too apparent.) Everywhere he turns, it seems, he comes face to face with his literary double.

> ...and when he asked another corrector the name of a book, on which he saw him at work; he understood it was the second part of the SAGE HIDALGO DON QUIXOTE DE LA MANCHA, written by a certain person, a native of Tordesillas. "I have heard of this performance, said the knight; and really, in my conscience, thought it was, long before this time, burned into ashes, or pounded into dust.... Works of the imagination are the more useful and entertaining, the nearer they approach the truth, and the more probability they contain; and, even history is valued according to its truth and authenticity." (2,62)

In real life, this spurious *Don Quixote* prodded Cervantes to finish the second part of his great book. In the novel, it prompts Quixote to change his plans (instead of going to Saragossa, he heads for Barcelona) and causes him immense anxiety. I have already mentioned the strange, sad scene near the end of the book (2,72) in which Quixote meets a man named Don Alvaro Tarfe whom he remembers seeing mentioned in the pages of the spurious *Don Quixote*. Tarfe claims that that Don Quixote "was an intimate acquaintance of mine." Sancho and his master protest and manage to convince Tarfe that he is mistaken or "inchanted." But, shaken, Quixote begs him for a written testimonial:

"...signor Don Alvaro Tarfe, I am the real Don Quixote de la Mancha, so well known to fame, and not that wretched impostor who has thought proper to usurp my name, and deck himself with the spoils of my reputation. I must therefore intreat your worship as you value yourself on the character of a gentleman, to make a declaration before the alcalde of the place; importing, that, before this day, you never saw me in the whole course of your life; and that I am not the Don Quixote described in the second part, nor this Sancho Panza the squire whom your worship knew in his service."

Note the sublime game Cervantes is playing here. This passage implies that beyond the spurious text there is actually a double, a fake Don Quixote, wandering about Spain on which the spurious text is based, and that Tarfe is both real and a character in a book (or a character in a book who has come to life). Tarfe replies:

"With all my heart...; and yet I cannot help being astonished to see two Don Quixotes, and two Sanchos at the same time, so familiar in name, and so unlike in character; so that I say again, and even affirm, that I have not really seen that which I thought I had seen, not met with those incidents in which I supposed myself concerned."

On one level this passage looks as if it's about appearance and reality, the novel's theme, according to received wisdom. But actually it's about personal identity, nominalism, language and logic. Tarfe is a character in a book who has encountered a logical paradox (a double), as is Quixote himself for that matter. This can only happen to characters in books because in real life certain laws of logic and identity obtain (e.g. two things cannot occupy the same space at the same time; the same thing cannot be in two places at once). If this were to happen to someone in real life (which it can't), that person would react exactly as Tarfe does; his own concept of personal identity would explode, he would doubt who he was and the ownership of his experiences. Once again Cervantes is manipulating the conventions of fiction to play with language itself. The effect is one of humour mixed with an immense existential sadness and despair. Quixote feels himself losing his sense of self, which, on a psychological level is akin to the despair of the clinically insane or the depression of the Alzheimer's patient who knows that his memories are slipping away.

Typically, Cervantes twists the scene's tail one more time before they all troop off to the alcalde to sign the deposition asserting their reality. Sancho pipes up, somewhat dryly: "Doubtless...your worship must be inchanted, like my lady Dulcinea del Toboso...." Sancho, of course, knows there is no Dulcinea and that she is not enchanted. So what he means is the precise opposite of what he says; like Dulcinea, Tarfe is not enchanted and he is not even real. He is only a thing made of words.

Arriving in Barcelona a few days before this, the old knight appeared to receive a warm welcome. But that evening his jocular hosts persuaded him to parade through streets in a heavy coat astride a mule instead of Rozinante. On the back of the coat they pinned a parchment sign: THIS IS DON QUIXOTE DE LA MANCHA.

Rozinante's Sex Life and Other Jokes

Don Quixote, besides being ineffably sad, is an extremely funny book. Cervantes' comic invention is as astonishing as it is infinite (yet, next to the book itself, any discussion of its humour will seem lame and unfunny: a paradox). In Volume 1, Chapter 15, Don Quixote and Sancho sit down for a picnic lunch in the open. Rozinante, till now so frail and decorous as to be beyond suspicion of sexual desire, is allowed to graze without a hobble. But the old horse smells some nearby mares and trots over eagerly "to communicate his occasions to the objects of his desire." The mares kick and bite him. Their Yanguesian masters run up with staves and beat him till his saddle falls off and he drops to the ground "almost battered to death." Don Quixote cheerfully observes to Sancho that since the Yanguesians are not knights Sancho can join him in taking revenge, a prospect which Sancho views without relish, observing that there are in fact twenty against two or "one and a half." Nevertheless, Sancho and Quixote attack and are beaten nearly to death with staves (note the parallel action).

What follows is a gorgeously comic dialogue scene (sounds like something written by Samuel Beckett): horse, knight and squire flat on the ground, unable to move anything but their mouths in speech (well, except for Rozinante, who suffers mutely throughout). Sancho wonders, "In how many days does your worship think we will be able to move our feet?" Don Quixote answers, in his usual tone of dignified tranquillity, "With regard to myself, I really cannot fix any number of days." And then he goes on to take the blame for their beating. He is being punished, Quixote thinks, for having transgressed the laws of chivalry by allowing himself to be drawn into battle with men who haven't been knighted. This is exactly the same sort of after-the-fact twisted logic Quixote uses throughout the novel to excuse his defeats and humiliations. After some back and forth, Sancho turns to the subject of the horse. "See if your worship can make shift to rise, and then we will give some assistance to Rozinante, tho' it be more than he deserves; for, he is the principal cause of all this plaguy ribroasting: never could I believe such a thing of Rozinante, who, I always thought, was as chaste and sober a person as myself: but, this verifies the common remark, that you must keep company a long time with a man, before you know him thoroughly; and that there is nothing certain in this life." At length, Sancho manages to get up and then help the horse to its feet. He puts Quixote over his donkey and ties the horse to the donkey's tail and heads for a nearby inn, which Quixote recognizes instantly as a castle.

This chapter is a set-piece version of the whole novel in a different key (to borrow Madariaga's metaphor). In this case, the old horse doubles for the old don, trotting out eagerly and surprisingly to meet the mares only to be bludgeoned at once for his pertinacity. This violent downfall is funny enough, funny in its sudden reversal of fortune and high hopes (high hopes that are funny in themselves being situated in the person of an old nag). But then Quixote and Sancho rush in with a similar eagerness and achieve a parallel fate. The dialogue that follows is comic in the way its dreamy tranquillity of tone contrasts with the physical circumstances of the characters—two men and a horse, prostrate, paralyzed, bruised, bleeding, suffering. The two men respond exactly as we have come to expect them to respond: Quixote with his self-serving logic and Sancho with his repertoire of long-suffering folk wisdom (only this time directed at a recumbent horse). Both men are entirely too philosophical in their predicament.

Nabokov calls the humour cruel, which seems strange coming from the man who wrote *Pnin* and *Lolita*. Evidently, his experience of American culture never extended to watching Coyote and Roadrunner cartoons on Saturday morning TV, or perhaps, when he put on his lecturer's cap, his personality turned ever so slightly grumpy and priggish. In any case, Cervantes' humour is violent, slapstick, earthy and, yes, cruel. The book is about disillusionment, it's about people laughing at someone else's naive hopes; there is nothing more cruel in life than losing hope. But it's also a cartoon of a book, hyperbolic and sudden in its deflation of tenderer moments and sentiments. Quixote doesn't just become disillusioned; he gets hit on the head with a two-by-four, over and over again (or he hits someone else on the head, often Sancho). And just as often, he bounces back up again, seemingly unscathed. It takes him 800 pages to begin to get the message.

There are three standard theories of the way humour works: 1) Henri Bergson's idea that repetitive (mechanical) behaviour is comic; 2) Mikhail Bakhtin's idea that humour derives from the juxtaposition of high (authoritative) and low (subversive) elements; and 3) a kind of Freudian notion that humour derives its power from latency—the joke is always on us and expresses what we fear most but don't want to face (illness, humiliation, sex and death are the top candidates). It doesn't really matter which theory one chooses in the case of *Don Quixote* since they all seem operative, often simultaneously. The old don's adventuring is compulsively mechanical; he's like one of those Energizer battery bunnies in rusty armour. His high flown sentiments are always being skewered by real events, often in the form of some violent come-uppance, or by Sancho's peasant logic, or simply by the ironic juxtaposition of another point of view. And there is plenty of evidence that one of Quixote's driving forces is a terror of sex (his invention of the ideal Dulcinea as a screen for the "hale, buxom" Aldonza, his hilarious bedroom scenes with Maritornes and the old duenna he thinks is Altisidora). In the encounter between Rozinante and the Yanguesian mares, the novel's latent sexual content comes closest to the surface, albeit in the character of a horse.

Aside from these broad categories of comedic structure, one can easily find at least seven types of humour used over and over again in *Don Quixote*: verbal, dialogic, reverse-trend, situational, slapstick, Rabelaisian, and parodic. (Certainly, there are others, but this is a rough sketch, not an exhaustive analysis.)

1) Verbal: I am least competent to judge the verbal comedy in the novel, which, as Nabokov observes, is the first thing we lose in a translation. Smollett gives the flavour best in the passages involving Sancho's constant mangling of highbrow words.

> "Signor, said the squire, I have at length traduced my wife to consent that I shall attend your worship wheresoever you shall please to carry me." "Say reduced, and not traduced, Sancho," replied the knight. "I have once or twice, if my memory serves me, said Sancho, intreated your worship, not to correct my words, if you understand my meaning; and when you can't make it out, I desire you would say, Sancho, or devil, I don't understand thee: then, if I fail in explaining myself, you may correct me as much as you please; for, I am so fossil." "I do not understand thee now, cried Don Quixote, nor can I comprehend what thou wouldst be at, in saying I am so fossil." "So fossil, said the squire; that is, whereby, as how I am just so." "Nay, now, thou art more and more unintelligible," replied the knight. "If your worship does not understand me now, answered Sancho, I know not how to express it; for, I am already at my wit's-end, and Lord have mercy upon me." "O! now I concéive thy meaning, said the knight; thou wouldst say thou art so docile, gentle and tractable, as to comprehend everything I say, and retain whatsoever I shall teach you." "I'll lay a wager, said the squire, that from the beginning, you know my meaning by my mumping, but wanted to confound me, by leading me into a thousand more blunders." "It may be so, said the knight.... (2,7)

Cervantes makes a lovely echo of passages such as this in conversations Sancho has with his wife Teresa Panza.

"I really do not understand you, said Teresa, you may do what you will; but, seek not to distract my brain with rhetorick and harranguing; for, if you be revolved to do what you say—" "You must call it resolved, woman, and not revolved," cried Sancho.... (2,5)

And there are dozens of sly little throwaways like the following (Sancho is speaking):

...and the true Don Quixote de la Mancha, the renowned, the valiant, the sage, the enamoured knight, the undoer of wrongs, the tutor of wards and orphans, the protector of widows, the destroyer of maids.... (2,72)

Or this passage in which the authorial first-person narrator wittily ridicules the world of chivalric romances.

...and protect those damsels who stroll about with whip and palfrey, from hill to hill, and from dale to dale, on the strength of their virginity alone: for, in times past, unless some libidinous clown with hatchet and morrion, or monstrous giant, forced her to his brutal wishes, a damsel might have lived fourscore years, without ever lying under any other cover than that of heaven, and then gone to her grave as good a maiden as the mother who bore her. (1,9)

But none of these translated passages, I suspect, come close to resurrecting the constant, delicate verbal play of the original Spanish. As Quixote himself says, a translation is "like the wrong side of Flemish tapestry, in which, tho' we distinguish the figures, they are confused and obscured by ends and threads, without the smoothness and expression which the other side exhibits." (2,62) Let me briefly try to give a taste of what is lost. In Volume 1, after arriving in the Sierra Morena, Quixote writes a letter to his beloved Dulcinea and sends Sancho to deliver it. The letter goes like this:

"Sovereign and sublime princess,
He who is wounded by the edge of absence, and whose heart is stuck full of the darts of affliction, most divine Dulcinea del Toboso! wishes thee that health which he is not doomed to enjoy. I am scorned by thy beauty, if thy virtue afford me no relief, if thy disdain completes my

misfortune; albeit, I am inured to suffering, I can ill support the misery I bear, which hath not only been excessive, but also of long duration. My trusty squire Sancho will give thee an ample relation, O ungrateful beauty and lovely foe! of the situation in which I remain on thy account: if it be thy will to succour me, I am thy slave; if not, use thy pleasure; for, the end of my life will satisfy thy cruelty and my desire. Thine till death,
The knight of the rueful countenance." (1,25)

Sancho forgets to bring the letter with him and a few pages later endeavours to recite it from memory for the curate and the barber whom he has met at a nearby inn.

"'Fore God! Mr. Licentiate, said he, I believe the devil has run away with every word that I remembered of his letter: tho' I am positive it began with 'subterrene and sublime princess!'" "It could not be subterrene, said the barber, but superterrene or sovereign." "You are in the right, resumed Sancho: then, if my memory does not fail me, it went on with 'the smitten, the sleepless and the sore, kisses your hands, most ungrateful and unregarded beauty:' and something or other of health and distemper which he wished her; running on at this rate, till he concluded with, Yours, till death, the knight of the rueful countenance." (1,26)

Now this is pretty funny, but Leo Spitzer, in his essay "Linguistic Perspectivism in *Don Quixote*," discusses the Spanish version of these passages in a way that partially illuminates the extraordinary phonological playfulness of the prose.

In this way, "soberana y alta señora [supreme and great lady]" becomes "alta y sobajada señora [great and crumpled lady]"—which the barber corrects to "...sobrehumana o soberana [...superhuman and supreme]": for this single term of address we are presented with three versions, resulting in a polyonomasia, as in the case of the proper names. Again, "de punto de ausencia y el llagado de las telas del corazon [from the place of absence and the wound of the heart's tissues} > "el llego y falto de sueño y el ferido [the arrival and lack of sleep and the wound] (it is as though Sancho, while indulging in Isidorian etymologies, is shrewdly diagnosing his master). (Spitzer, *Miguel de Cervantes, Modern Critical Views*, 22)

2) Dialogic: Cervantes was a playwright as well as a novelist so that his dialogue is always terrific, combining character driven speeches, precise tonal variation, irony and dramatic structure to make the dialogue scenes work on several levels simultaneously. Sometimes he outdoes himself though. Sometimes he seems to have invented Monty Python sketches four centuries ahead of schedule (or is this a Spanish version of a borscht-belt stand-up comedy routine?). One can almost hear the voice of John Cleese in the rhythms and absurdities of the following:

> They retired to their chamber, and supper-time approaching, Sancho desired to know what they could have for that meal? To this interrogation mine host replied, that his taste should be fitted to a hair, and that he might bespeak what he liked best; for, as far as the birds of the air, the fowls of the land, and the fish of the sea could go, he would find the house provided. "Less than all that will serve, answered Sancho: we shall be satisfied with a couple of chickens roasted; for, my master has a very delicate taste, and eats little; and, as for myself, I am not a very unconscionable cormorant."
>
> The other frankly owned he had not chickens; for, the kites had destroyed the brood. "Well then, Mr. Landlord, said the squire, you may order a pullet to be put to the fire; but, see it be very tender." "A pullet! cried the inn-keeper: body of my father! now, as I'm an honest man, I sent about half an hundred yesterday to market: but, setting aside pullets, you may have what you will." "If that be the case, said Sancho, there will be no want of veal or kid." "At present, replied the inn-keeper, there is really none in the house: we are just out of these articles; but, next week, we shall have enough and to spare." "To be sure, we shall be much the better for that, answered Sancho: I'll lay a wager all these wants will be supplied with plenty of eggs and

bacon." "'Fore God! said the host, my guest has an admirable knack at guessing: I have told him there is neither hen nor pullet in the house, and he would have me treat him with eggs! Shift about, if you please, to some other delicacies, and think no more of poultry."

"Body o' me! cried Sancho, let us come to some resolution; tell me at once what is in the house, and pray, Mr. Landlord, no more of your shiftings." "What I really and truly can afford, said the inn-keeper, is a dish of cow-heel...." (2,59)

3) Reverse-trend: As I say, much of the continuing humour of the novel falls into the Bergsonian category of robotic behaviour. Quixote just keeps repeating the same mistakes over and over again. But some of the most delightful lines in the novel come when Quixote reverses the general trend and shows himself, to the surprise and consternation of the other characters, to be perfectly capable of judging a situation correctly. In Volume 1, Chapter 30, there is a lovely instance of this: Dorotea, pretending to be the Princess Micomicona, is blathering on glibly (she's a bit of an airhead) to Don Quixote about how she came from Africa in search of a famous knight to free her kingdom from its giant oppressor when she makes an elementary mistake in geography.

"...and I have exactly followed his directions, in recommending my cause to the protection of signor Don Quixote, who is certainly the individual knight my father described; since his features correspond with his fame, which fills not only Spain, but, likewise the whole province of la Mancha; for, scarce had I landed at Ossuna, than hearing of his vast exploits, my mind suggested that he must be the very person I came in quest of." "How could your highness, said Don Quixote, land at Ossuna, which is not a sea-port?"

Perhaps equally funny, but also very complex and shot through with sadness, is the moment when Sancho tries to convince Quixote that three peasant girls on donkeys are none other than Dulcinea del Toboso and two of her ladies-in-waiting.

By this time, they were clear of the wood, and in sight of the three country-maidens; when the knight lifting up his eyes, and surveying the whole road to Toboso, without seeing anything but them, began to be troubled in mind, and asked Sancho, if the ladies had got out of town when he left them. "Out of town! said Sancho. What? are your worship's eyes in the nape of your neck, that you don't see them coming towards us, glittering and shining like the sun at noon?" "I see no body, replied the knight, but three country wenches riding upon asses." "God deliver me from the devil! cried the squire, is it possible that three bellfreys, or how-d'ye-call-ums, white as the driven snow, should appear no better than asses, in your worship's eyes? By the lord! I'll give you leave to pluck off every hair of my beard, if that be the case." "Then I tell thee, Sancho, said his master, they are as certainly he or she-asses as I am Don Quixote, and thou Sancho Panza, at least, so they seem to me." (2,10)

Sancho Panza has moments of ironic reversal as well. Near the beginning of Volume 2 he has a long conversation with his wife about setting out again with Quixote (partly quoted above in the context of verbal humour). He speaks in such elevated tones and "in a stile quite different from that which might be expected from his shallow understanding" that the Portuguese translator (of Cid Hamet's Arabic manuscript) believes the whole chapter must be apocryphal (2,5). And later, when the Duke endows Sancho with an island, the squire, to the surprise of his sham court, turns out to be a shrewd and able administrator, and never moreso than when he chooses to resign his governorship in order to remain true to himself. "All the company embraced him, and were in their turns embraced by the weeping Sancho, who left them equally astonished at his discourse, as at his resolute, and wise determination." (2,53)

4) Situational: I call the comedy situational when its effect depends on a discrepancy between what a character thinks is going on and what his situation really is. In *Don Quixote*, this generally happens in one of two ways. Either the old don, through his chivalric delusions and hobbyhorses, misreads the real situation, e.g. sheep are enemy

knights, or he is the victim of some trick, as in the confidence games practiced by the curate and Dorotea or the Duke and the Duchess or the attempted seduction by Altisidora. Of course, most of the examples of these types of humour are actually mixed, using two or more strategies simultaneously, but there are literally dozens of scenes involving situational humour in the novel.

Take, as examples, the novel's two great parallel bedroom scenes. In Volume 1, Chapter 16, during Quixote's first night at the miraculous inn of crossed-plots, he is put to bed in a sort of attic dormitory along with Sancho and a mule driver. Quixote thinks the inn is a castle. He can't sleep because his bruises ache (from a previous encounter) and because of an alarming situation he believes himself involved in.

> This was no other than...that the landlord's daughter was the governor's only child, who, captivated by his genteel appearance, was become deeply enamoured of him, and had actually promised to come, without the knowledge of her parents, and pass the best part of the night in bed with him...he began to reflect with extreme anxiety, upon the dangerous dilemma into which his virtue was like to be drawn; and resolved in his heart, to commit no treason against his mistress Dulcinea del Toboso; even tho' queen Ginebra herself, and the lady Qintaniona should make him a tender of their favours.

Unknown to him, Maritornes, the tavern bicycle, has made an assignation with the mule driver. She ascends the ladder and enters the attic. Feeling her way in the dark, she brushes by Quixote who grabs her by the wrist and drags her into bed, believing

> ...he folded in his arms the goddess of beauty, and straining her in his embrace, began to pronounce, in soft and amorous tone, "Would to heaven! I were so circumstanced, beautiful and high-born lady! as to be able to repay the transcendent favour bestowed upon me, in the contemplation of your amazing charms....

What follows is a catastrophe. Maritornes raises the alarm. The mule driver punches Quixote so hard it "bathed his whole countenance in blood." Maritornes feels her way in the dark into Sancho's bed. Sancho thinks he's having a nightmare and punches Maritornes who starts punching him back. The mule driver comes to her rescue and the inn-keeper comes with a candle to punish her. The candle goes out.

And so on....

The comedy of the scene depends upon Quixote's fevered and obsessional misreading of the situation which triggers a sequence of slapstick misunderstandings. In the parallel scenes in Volume 2, Altisidora pretends to fall in love with Quixote in order to entertain the Duke and Duchess with his reactions to his predicament. When he overhears her talking of love in the garden beneath his bedroom window,

> ...his imagination was instantly filled with an infinity of similar adventures of rails and gardens, serenades, court-ships and swoonings, which he had read in his vain books of chivalry: and he concluded that some damsel of the dutchess was enamoured of him, but that modesty com-pelled her to keep her inclinations secret. Possessed of this notion, he began to be afraid of his virtue; but, he resolved, in his own mind, to hold out to the last.... (2,44)

Four chapters later, he hears a key turning in the lock of his bed-room door "and straight imagined the enamoured damsel was come to surprize his chastity" (2,48). It isn't Altisidora, of course, but an ancient, bespectacled duenna, Donna Rodriguez, come to ask for his help. But at first Quixote thinks she's a ghost; then he thinks she's a go-between bringing messages from his seductress; then he's afraid that being alone in a bedroom with a strange woman might "waken those desires in me which are now asleep, and compel me at these years to fall, where hitherto I have never so much as stumbled?" (2,48) He tries to lock her out of the bedroom, but then finds him-self face to face with her in his nightshirt. They both jump back; they're both afraid of "assault and ravishment." The old woman asks Quixote who he's afraid of.

> "Of you, and from you, and you alone, answered Don Quixote: for, I am not made of marble, nor you of brass; nor is it now ten o'clock in the forenoon, but midnight, and something more, if I am not mistaken, and we are here

in a more close and secret apartment than the cave in which
the treacherous, and daring Aeneas, enjoyed the beautiful
and pious Dido...." (2,48)

But then he pulls himself together and with great courtesy kisses
her hand, leads her to a chair at the foot of his bed and jumps under
the covers, gathering them close so there is nothing showing but his
face. And she begins to tell her story.

It's a gorgeous, gentle, hilarious scene built on Altisidora's fake
seduction and the connivance of the court, the old don's own obsessional thinking, and his fear for his chastity (that latent sexual
content). The two old people in their nightgowns, trembling for
their virtue, then sweetly walking hand in hand toward the bed are
irresistible. Even the Moorish narrator, Cid Hamet Benengeli,
cannot forego an interruption at this point. "Here Cid Hamet, in a
parenthesis, swears by Mahomet, that to have seen these two origi-
nals thus linked, and walking from the door to the bed, he would
have given the best of his two jackets."

5) Slapstick: Pain is funny (despite what Nabokov says). Humiliation is funny. *Don Quixote* is full of rough, physical humour, banana
peel pratfalls and cartoon beatings that make the old don and
Sancho look like precursors of the Three Stooges. I give just a
couple of instances. When Quixote meets the Duke and Duchess in
Volume 2, he rides over and tries to dismount in order to kiss the
lady's hand in a courtly manner. But the saddle slips and dumps
him on the ground.

Don Quixote approaching with his beaver up, made a
motion to alight, and Sancho made haste to hold the
stirrup; but, he was so unfortunate, that in dismounting
from Dapple, he slipped his foot through the noose of the
stirrup-rope, in such a manner, that he could not possibly
disentangle himself, but continued hanging with his face
and part of his body on the ground. The knight, who never
alighted without his assistance, imagining that Sancho, as
usual, held the stirrup, threw himself off with a swing, and
the saddle, which must have been very ill girted, and he,
came to the ground together; not without great disgrace,
and a thousand curses, which he muttered between his

teeth, against the unfortunate Sancho, whose leg was still in the stocks. (2,30)

I mentioned earlier the fact that rage is Don Quixote's most common response to an ill turn in the plot (odd how critics of the dreamy, sentimental school fail to notice this aspect of his character). More often than not he vents his rage on the nearest innocent bystander who is usually Sancho. For example,

> Don Quixote finding that Sancho made a jest of him, was so much provoked, that, lifting up his lance, he bestowed upon him two or three thwacks, which, had they fallen upon his head, as they lighted on his shoulders, would have saved his master the trouble of paying his salary.... (1,20)

And:

> Don Quixote was enraged, when he heard such blasphemies uttered against his mistress Dulcinea, and lifting up his lance, without speaking a syllable, or giving the least notice of his intention, discharged two such hearty blows upon the squire, as brought him instantly to the ground.... (1,30)

Or Quixote will smack someone else.

> "You are an impudent rascal! (cried the knight, overhearing what he said) it is your skull that is unfurnished and unfound; but, mine is more pregnant than the abominable whore that brought you forth." So saying, he snatched up a loaf, and flung it at the goatherd with such fury, that he levelled his nose with his face. (1,52)

Or someone else will knock Sancho on the head.

> So saying, he clapped his fingers to his nostrils, and began to bray so stoutly, that all the neighbouring vallies re-echoed the sound. But, one of those who stood next to him, supposing the squire made himself merry at their expence, lifted up a pole that was in his hand, and bestowed it upon him with such good will, that Sancho, in spite of all his efforts, came to the ground. (2,27)

6) Rabelaisian (humour of the low, bodily kind): This is the kind of humour Bakhtin discusses in his book *Rabelais and His World*, humour that derives much of its force from the implicit critique of one discourse (discourse of authority) by another (bodily discourse) placed next to it. The body is an awkward, embarrassing article, always betraying our noble ideals and intellectual pretensions. There are several moments in the novel in which shit, piss or vomit betray the old don and his squire. See, for example, the above-mentioned incidents involving the balsam of Fierabras (1,17 and 1,18) and the scene (1,49) in which Quixote has to go the bathroom but thinks he can't get out of the enchanted cage in order to do so in private. But the absolutely quintessential scene of this sort takes place just as Quixote and Sancho reach the Sierra Morena in Volume 1, Chapter 20. Darkness falls as they enter a broad valley with a fast-moving creek flowing through it. Suddenly they notice a horrible sound: "they heard the sound of regular strokes, accompanied with strange clanking of iron chains, which, added to the dreadful din of the cataract, would have smote the heart of any other but Don Quixote with fear and consternation."

Now the sound comes from a nearby fulling mill (for making felt), but neither the don nor Sancho realize this (nor does the reader, for that matter). Quixote thinks it's a giant and he prepares, heroically, to ride out and meet it. Sancho is terrified. He can't bear to face giants and, equally, he can't bear to be left alone in the dark. He surreptitiously ties Rozinante's legs together so that all the horse can do is hop awkwardly when Quixote spurs him forward. At the same time, Sancho grabs Quixote's saddle and refuses to let him go. Stuck together like that they spend the night in what to me is one of the most heroic and yet funniest scene sequences in the novel. Quixote really thinks there is some gruesome giant lurking just out of sight and he refuses to run away (and he never sleeps much anyway). Sancho's job in the scene is to be terrified and prevent the noble don from deeds of chivalry and martyrdom—something utterly symbolic (and Bakhtinian) right there.

But Cervantes intensifies the scene when Sancho, either from fear or in the natural course of events, suddenly realizes he has to defecate. He won't let go of his master lest they lose each other in the dark, and he's too embarrassed to mention what he needs to do.

...and therefore, to compromise the matter, he flipp'd his right hand from the hinder part of the saddle, and without any noise, softly undid the slip knot by which his breeches were kept up: and upon which, they of themselves fell down to his heels, where they remained like a pair of shackles; he then gathered up his shirt from behind, as well as he could; and exposed his posteriors, which were none of the smallest, to the open air: this being done, and he imagined it was the chief step he could take to deliver himself from the pressing occasion and dilemma, in which he was, another difficulty still greater occurred, namely, that he should not be able to disincumber himself without noise: he therefore, began to fix his teeth close, shrug up his shoulders, and hold in his breath with all his might. But, notwithstanding these precautions, he was so unlucky in the issue, as to produce a rumbling sound very different from that which had terrified him so much. It did not escape the ears of Don Quixote, who immediately cried, "What noise is that, Sancho?" "I know not, sir," said the squire, "it must be some new affair, for adventures and misadventures never begin with trifles." He tried his fortune a second time, and without any more noise or disorder, freed himself from the load which had given him so much uneasiness. But, as Don Quixote's sense of smelling, was altogether as acute as that of his hearing, and Sancho stood so close to him, that the vapours ascended towards him, almost in a direct line, he could not exclude some of them from paying a visit to his nose. No sooner was he sensible of the first salutation, than in his own defence, he pressed his nose between his finger and thumb, and in a snuffling tone, pronounced, "Sancho, thou seemest in great fear." (1,20)

(What one also realizes, looking at this and earlier examples, is how wonderfully cunning Cervantes is at stretching out a comic situation and then capping it with a gorgeous line of dialogue.)

7) Parodic: As I say, there are three general categories or sources of humour, and they all depend on a dyadic structure of juxtaposition

and antithesis. Comedy happens when a text challenges the reader to hold in mind simultaneously two contrasting images or modes of behaviour. What makes humour especially fascinating is the sense that in laughter we make an implicit judgment about healthy and unhealthy ways of conducting ourselves. We mentally juxtapose the obsessional or robotic behaviour of a character like Don Quixote with a more flexible, adaptive, realistic and ultimately intelligent way of dealing with the world. Or we mentally juxtapose his sententious and hyperbolic notions of chivalry with a more down-to-earth and pragmatic courtesy (which might involve realizing that other people have points of view, too). Or we mentally juxtapose the old don's sexual anxiety (all the worry about chastity in a 50-year-old man) with a more worldly and psychologically hygienic view of human sexual behaviour. We find relief (and release) in laughter because in making the implicit judgment we express our own health, intelligence and humanity. (This state of spiritual well-being lasts about as long as the laughter itself.)

Parody, on the other hand, has an interesting triangular structure, requiring the reader to hold three things in mind at once: the work in hand, the work being parodied and an imagined work that is neither one nor the other. (Parody makes us all imaginary writers as well as readers.) A text is ripe for parody as soon as it can be taken out of context or, perhaps, out of the author's control. All of a sudden what was wise seems bombastic, what was romantic seems sentimental and saccharine, what was brave seems foolishly risky, and what was tender seems naive and simple. The whole of *Don Quixote* is a parody of the chivalric romances that inspire the old don's adventures, most obviously *Amadis of Gaul* (the earliest version was written in the fourteenth century by the Portuguese author Vasco de Lobeira) and the adventures of Sir Lancelot in the Matter of Britain. The technique is to exaggerate the language and diminish the content. Quixote commits himself to titanic struggles with giants that turn out to be bags of wine, he embarks in a magic boat and gets dragged into a millrace, he wrestles to preserve his chastity against women who are completely uninterested him.

And yet, in the best parodies, there is always an element of love for that which is parodied. This is a special moment in the rise and fall of literary convention: an author, who can no longer reproduce a genre in its classical form, must mangle and skewer it as a kind of

67

reverse homage. But at certain moments the old form shines out, or flickers briefly into focus, purer, it seems, than ever. Speaking of Quixote's night of vigil over his armour before the water trough on his first expedition, Nabokov writes:

> It is here that the parody of chivalry becomes for the first time in the book lost in the pathetic, poignant, divine element which radiates from Don Quixote.... We are haunted by the creeping feeling that tables are being gently turned, and that these books [chivalric romances] and those dreams and that madness are of a finer quality—and, in a word, ethically better—than the curate's and the housekeeper's so-called common sense. (*Lectures on Don Quixote*, 42-43)

Thus in all instances the effect of the humour in *Don Quixote* is to extend the shifting structure of the novel as a whole (the nested narrators, the cascading points of view), inserting at each step fresh levels of relativism and a denial of surface meaning. Don Quixote is both the man who delivers eloquent, erudite and sweetly reasoned speeches in a voice that is as gentle as it is dignified and the man who attacks a goatherd with a loaf of bread with such violence that "he levelled his nose with his face." (1,52) The irony is subversive and pervasive. It makes one wonder what Cervantes does want the reader to take seriously. Don Quixote is both insane and a comic figure, his authority doubly negated. Every sentence in the book seems tongue-in-cheek, even those sentences that purport to tell us the book's purpose (something to do with disparaging chivalric romances). The effect is one of stunning fluidity. The reader's mind flows through successive states—pity, belief, disbelief, laughter—depending on whether a passage inspires him with sadness or suggests itself as a piece of existential wisdom or surprises him with an act of comic silliness that ironizes all the rest. This swooping fluidity (I am not going to use the word "flickering" for a while in order not to seem quite so obsessive as I probably am), this giving over control of one's own responses to the novel itself, may be the chief effect of a great book. It becomes less a vessel of meaning than an experience in itself, an experience that leaves the reader shivered and limp but with a sense that he has lived through a great time, a residue of feeling that seems, in some lights, like meaning.

Some Ancillary Devices

It may seem tedious to spend so much time on structural issues, on plot and subplot patterns, point of view, and the interplay of narrators, texts, irony, humour and language. But we do honour to the writer to try to have in mind as much of his novel as possible before making any deductions or leaping to any conclusions about it. It's important to spend some time looking steadily at just what the author did on the page because it's always the case with an author as wonderful as Cervantes that the closer we look, the better we read, the more complex, subtle and interesting the book becomes. And it is in the nature of a novel like *Don Quixote,* because of its proliferation of layers, parallels and reflective structures, that any one element is repeated, balanced, undercut, ironized, deformed or denied somewhere else in the book. It becomes less and less probable that any statement in the book can be taken to mean what it says it means, that the book itself is univocal. We need always to remember this. You can't read the book without reading the book.

And having summarized the story, analyzed the desire/ resistance structure of the plot, parsed the subplots, looked into the point-of-view layering, examined the nested narrators and books within books, and dissected the comedy, I still find that I have a long list of structures and devices that seem especially important to the novel. I can't possibly cover them all (that's why Cervantes wrote the novel). But here is a truncated sample, a taste. It's important to realize that these sorts of structures also constitute "action" in the novel, albeit an action that is grammatical and cerebral (action of sequence, association, juxtaposition, interconnection and delay) as opposed to what we normally think of as action, that is, character gesture.

1) The inset stories (Cervantes' version of TV soap operas with their interchangeable and generically gorgeous heroes and ingenues). Viktor Shklovsky is good on how these are integrated into the novel (*Theory of Prose*). He sees *Don Quixote* as a frame novel, the purpose of which is to contain the inset stories, much in the manner of Boccaccio's *Decameron* or Marguerite de Navarre's *Heptameron*. I'm not sure that I buy this, that somehow the structure of the novel as

a whole is subordinate to the inset pieces; this seems like a some-what over-simplified reading of the plot structure. And it seems clear that Cervantes himself changed the way he incorporated the inset stories from the first part of the novel to the second part. (I shall return to this subject later in the essay.)

In any case, there are a huge number of these inset stories— stories told to Don Quixote by people he meets along the way, stories read in found manuscripts ("The Impertinent Curiosity"), stories that are told to Quixote and then develop further as the characters interact around him, that is, in a sense, Quixote walks into and observes other characters' stories. There are also inset poems and songs, which tell yet more stories. To a certain extent, especially in Volume 1, the novel does begin to look like a hybrid construct, something part-way between a story collection and a novel. But I wonder if this view isn't motivated in part by a certain unexamined superiority of outlook based on historical perspective. We're later, so we know better. *Don Quixote* is earlier, therefore it must be primitive in some sense. And I think of the Australian author Murray Bail whose contemporary novel *Eucalyptus* is con-structed around the production of multiple inset stories. And then I think we should dig deeper.

In the normal course of events, the inset stories should work in two ways: a) as devices to delay and retard plot (Shklovsky's idea that a lot of the reason for aesthetic devices is to make the straight path crooked, to slow down and make strange the experience of the story); and b) to support, reinforce and reflect the main plot and theme (and thus they are a reflective device related to subplot and set-piece). Now these stories do delay the plot, sure enough, but the common objection (as mentioned in the novel itself) to them is that they do not relate to the main plot. But a very useful mental exper-iment is to take an argument and run the logic backwards to see if a different or more illuminating answer comes out.

In this case, the conventional argument runs that *Don Quixote* is about the clash between fantasy (Quixote) and realism (Sancho). All the inset stories are about love, so clearly they are off topic and irrelevant. But if you run the argument backwards, it goes like this: all the inset stories are about love, therefore the main plot of the novel is about love, or at least it's more about love than it is about the conflict between fantasy and realism (often in good, complex novels there seems to be more than one simple theme; this is commonly a problem of hierarchy—the themes will be found to be arranged as sub-themes and analogous themes). And in Volume 2, many of the inset stories are about lovers who fall under an enchantment—a clear parallel to the enchanted Dulcinea theme on the main plot line.

What we can say is that there might be a way of constructing a reading of the novel in which the inset stories, being on romantic themes, are much closer to the main theme of the novel than critics generally assume. Taken together they seem concerned with many of the basic love issues in Western culture: love in conflict with parental wishes, love across class boundaries, jealousy, revenge, love across racial or ethnic boundaries, seduction without love. Several stories hang on a concept of betrothal (almost a spiritual pre-marriage) that seems a bit strange to us; in these stories a certain sort of avowal of love accompanied by sex is tantamount to a binding marriage contract; in the course of the story, this contract will get broken in one way or another (the seducer moves on to another woman, parents force a different marriage on their children, etc.); and then somehow the right (pre-married) couples end up with each other.

This doesn't mean true love always wins out. For example, Dorotea ends up with her seducer, not necessarily a man to inspire real love (although Cervantes gives us the sense that he might grow into his marriage). In the inset novella "The Impertinent Curiosity" in Volume 1, on the other hand, a man's jealousy destroys his marriage. In Volume 2, Chapter 60, we find the story of Claudia Geronima: she is betrothed, but her lover appears to abandon her for another; she kills him only to find out that she was mistaken. Again jealousy destroys a marriage (Nabokov calls this episode "idiotic"). And there are two inset stories involving Arabs and Christians. In Volume 1, it's the story of a captured Christian escaping North Africa with his Arab sweetheart; in Volume 2, it's a story involving a Morisco, a Christianized Arab girl who has been expelled from Spain, escaping from North Africa with her Spanish lover on a Turkish brigantine. It's fascinating to note how, over and over, when he can, Cervantes mirrors motifs in Volume 1 and Volume 2, how heavily patterned the novel is. Like any good novelist, he is obsessive in his multiplication of thematic and structural mirrors.

71

One more lovely example: during Quixote's sojourn with the Duke and Duchess, two of the inset "duenna" stories have to do with enchanted lovers which repeat the enchantment motif on the main Quixote-Dulcinea plot line.

What one notices is that these inset stories form a network of themes, plot concerns and motifs that actually seem remarkably consistent and focused. At the same time, they are presented as variations on a theme, arabesque embellishments that seem oddly artificial (or idiotic, as Nabokov says) and much less interested than the rest of the novel in achieving qualities we expect in a modern novel, especially verisimilitude, the quality of seeming to be real. They sometimes seem hasty, especially in Volume 2, sketched in (for example, the story of Ricote's Morisco daughter and her lover) —which makes me wonder if, to Cervantes, the idea of the inset story, the example, was more important than spelling out the narrative elaboration. Rather than being about love, precisely, they often seem concentrated on that moment of betrothal, the marriage contract, and the things that interfere with the proper follow through. Again it might not be safe to draw a conclusion; as I keep saying, better to take note and keep the idea in play. And there is much more to be said on the whole subject of the inset stories.

2) The speeches and intellectual byplay (dialogues, debates). Periodically Quixote gets up on his soap box and delivers a speech. Often Sancho is his only audience. These aren't soliloquies or public orations before large groups of people; they are more like little essays in dialogue. For example, in Volume 1, Chapter 11, Quixote discourses to the goatherds on the Golden Age (Quixote tends to take a romantic view of rural pursuits). Shklovsky says this speech is cribbed from Ovid. In Volume 1, Chapter 13, he encounters two gentlemen on horseback and six shepherds (dressed in black sheepskin jackets, garlanded with cypress and bitter-bay, and carrying holly clubs in their hands—note the precise details). To them, he delivers an address on knight-errantry, tracing its roots to the legendary King Arthur and the Round Table. In Volume 1, Chapter 37, he interrupts dinner to launch into a comparison of the military and scholarly professions. In Volume 1, Chapters 49 and 50, after being let out of the "enchanted" cage to relieve himself, Quixote gets into conversation with a canon (he has joined the

curate and the barber on their homeward journey; Quixote, as I say, is travelling in the cage). Quixote discourses at length on chivalric romances and the writing of fiction. In Volume 2, Chapter 6, he delivers a speech to his niece on families, lineage, good breeding and happiness. Two chapters later, he natters on to Sancho about fame and celebrity. In the late chapter mentioned above wherein Quixote visits a printing shop, we find a speech on translation theory. Sometimes, though rarely and usually when Quixote is not on the scene, other people make speeches: for example, when the curate and the barber sort through Quixote's library (1,6) or at the end of Volume 1 when the curate and the canon get into a discussion of chivalric romances and popular theatre (1,48).

These are just some examples of the speeches in the novel. Of course, like the inset stories, they are devices of delay; they get in the way of the plot. And often they turn on a subject matter related to the concerns of the novel: knight-errantry, chivalric romances, honour, etc. Also, as Shklovsky points out, Cervantes developed a lovely ironic thread contrasting Quixote's insanity, his mania, his folly, with his ability to discourse intelligently and even wisely on all sorts of subjects, much to the surprise of people he meets along the way who expect him to be crazy and stupid (much the way Sancho surprises everyone by his sage and judicious governance when he's given a town to run). For example,

> The canon could not help gazing at him, being struck with admiration, at the strange unaccountable symptoms of his disorder; for, in all his conversation and replies, he gave evident proofs of an excellent understanding, and never lost himself, except on the subject of chivalry, as we have formerly observed: he was therefore touched with compassion for his infirmity.... (1,49)

Like any good author, Cervantes is constantly manipulating expectation and variation to surprise the reader and keep him interested. In this case, the lines just cited occur as Quixote walks into the bushes to relieve himself. When he returns, the canon and the old don sit down together for a picnic and a talk, which is interrupted when Quixote loses his temper and attacks a goatherd "with such fury, that he levelled his nose to his face" (for some reason, this is one of my favourite lines in the book). Then he mounts Rozinante and attacks a religious procession (and gets beaten to a pulp). Pattern: sensible literary discussion bracketed by Rabelaisian potty humour and comic violence.

One tends to think that speeches and debates are a slightly dated compositional technique, and perhaps that is so. But it's interesting to look at a movie (the last place, I suppose, one would think to look) like *Four Weddings and a Funeral* where we find a pattern of speeches used in a similar way, to mark an ironic distinction between wisdom and foolishness. The speeches are about love and marriage, which connects with the thematics of the movie. And they work dialectically, as a sequence, each speech contrasting with and a response to the ones before.

Cervantes seems quite aware that he is creating a pattern: for example, when Quixote goes off on soldiers and scholars at dinner (1,37), Cervantes carefully inserts a tie-back line connecting this speech with the speech to the goatherds (1,11). "...when Don Quixote, leaving off eating, and inspired by the same spirit that moved him to harangue among the goatherds, began the following dissertation:....." This indicates how aware he was of the need to create connections between passages across the fabric of the book. Shklovsky observes:

> This allusion by Cervantes to an earlier speech along similar lines is most curious. Likewise, in the critical passages incorporated into *Don Quixote* (the examination of Don Quixote's library, the conversation with the innkeeper, and so on) we hear mention of the housekeeper who had burned the knight's books—the first act of criticism.
>
> In the complex novelistic schemata of our new age, the relationship between kindred episodes is achieved by the repetition of certain words, very much in the manner of Wagnerian leitmotivs.... (*Theory of Prose*, 74)

3) Set-pieces. Set-pieces are more or less self-contained units of narrative that repeat or reflect the structure of the whole or some crucial aspect of the whole. In this it reproduces the resonating effect of a subplot, though a subplot recurs and develops through time, whereas a set-piece happens only once. For example, the wonderful steeplechase chapter in *Anna Karenina* is a set-piece.

Vronsky, ever headstrong and careless, rides his little mare to death in the race. Anna, seated with her bureaucrat husband in the stands, looks on in horror. Karenin, with a cold eye, watches Anna watching Vronsky. Tolstoy explicitly links Anna and the mare in the text. The incident repeats the crucial pattern of relationships that drive Anna to kill herself at the end of the novel. And the mare's death, even the manner of her dying, explicitly foreshadows the death of the protagonist.

In a certain light, many of the incidents in *Don Quixote* qualify as versions of the set-piece device in that they repeat the pattern of the whole work: naive and obsessional hero mistakes situation, acts accordingly, and meets disaster (the battle of the windmills, the battle of the wine-skins, Rozinante's dalliance with the Yanguesian mares, the night of the fulling mill, etc.—a very long list). But there are a few incidents that seem to go beyond a mere recapitulation of the arc of action. They seem luminous with a sense of larger meaning and signal the prophetic quality on which the novel's greatness stands.

To pick just three: Volume 2, Chapter 11, in which Quixote encounters Death (Sancho and Quixote meet a troupe of actors on the road, in a moment of ironic reversal Quixote quickly realizes the truth of the situation and refrains from attacking, then a clown comes up and pretends to attack him, causes Rozinante to rear and throw Quixote on the ground and steals Dapple); Volume 2, Chapter 26, in which Quixote assaults a puppet show (in the midst of a puppet show representing a battle between the heroic knight Don Gayferos and an army of Moors—a story of chivalry and romance of precisely the kind that drove Quixote insane in the first place, he mutates from spectator to critic to participant, destroying the puppets with his sword, then blaming those "inchanters" when convinced of his mistake); and Volume 2, Chapter 58, in which Quixote views a series of carvings depicting warrior saints.

This last bears a closer look. It's less than two pages long and yet is a lovely example of a classical Greek device called the epyllion.

> The digression is a second story...contained within the first, and frequently unconnected with the subject. Usually, it appears as a story told by one of the characters; less

commonly as a description of a work of art. Judging from the extant examples, it seems to have been the practice to secure an artistic connection between the two parts of the poem by using parallel subjects and contrasting details.... The Shield of Achilles and the narrative of Odysseus are obvious Homeric examples. (Marjorie Crump, *The Epyllion from Theocritus to Ovid*, 23-24)

Sancho and Quixote are riding along when they come upon a group of workmen taking lunch in the open. They are transporting four carved images for an altar to be set up in a nearby town. One by one they unveil the images for Quixote to admire. They include St. George spearing a dragon, St. Martin "on horseback, dividing his cloak with a beggar," St. James (San Diego) trampling the Moors, and St. Paul falling from his horse at the moment of his conversion—all soldier saints, according to Quixote, who "conquered heaven by the force of their arms; for, heaven may be won by force."

The scene is written sweetly, without violence or slapstick. The old don observes that the difference between these men and himself is that they were saints and he is a sinner who has thus far in his adventures accomplished little of consequence. But the implication of the epyllion structure is to tie Quixote firmly together with the soldier saints, that like them he is on a mission to storm heaven itself. And he himself feels transformed, suddenly hopeful again, by the experience of seeing the images. Even the workmen are "astonished at the knight's appearance and discourse." So that Cervantes achieves here another of those luminous moments when the old knight's purity of heart, his own saintliness, radiates from the page.

4) Folk wisdom. This is an aspect of the book that sometimes reminds me of Flaubert's project of compiling a dictionary of bourgeois clichés. The sheer number of folk sayings, proverbs and old saws Cervantes throws down on the page is amazing. It bespeaks a systematic effort to collect and compile or at the very least an incredibly good ear and memory. At first, he puts most of these in Sancho's mouth and it looks as if one of the contrasts he's making is between the conventionalized folk wisdom of the illiterate peasant and the high flown intellectual discourse of his master. Later in the novel, as Quixote's fantasy world begins to fall apart, he sometimes

breaks into proverbs just as Sancho begins to speak like a man of measured intellect. (I have already mentioned the chapter the Portuguese translator believed to be apocryphal because he didn't expect Sancho to speak so well. (2,25))

Nabokov says most of the power of these Breughel-esque passages is lost in translation, which may be true. They do form a consistent armature of the Quixote-Sancho dialogue system. That is, the two are like a pair of stand-up comedy actors with a routine. Sancho runs a string of proverbs; Quixote figuratively slaps his hand over his brow. This goes on throughout the book with some variation: sometimes Quixote will speak in proverbs and Sancho will accuse him of being hypocritical. As I say, this is just one armature of a larger system involving discourse imbalances. For example, Sancho is also always mangling his diction, picking unlikely homonyms or making awful puns. Quixote (figuratively slapping his hand over his brow) corrects him. Then, delightfully, Sancho proceeds to correct his wife, who makes the same sort of language errors.

Here are a couple of passages, just to give a taste:

"As for my own part, said Sancho, I neither say nor think any such thing; those that do may dine upon it: if they were too familiar, by this time they have answered for it to God. I prune my own vine, and know nothing about thine. I never meddle with other people's concerns. He that buys and denies, his own purse belies; as the saying is. Bare I was born, and bare I remain: and if I lose nothing, as little I gain. If he did lie with her that is no matter of mine. Many people hunt the hare without ever finding the scut; for, Til you hedge in the sky, the starlings will fly. And evil tongues will not refrain from God himself."

"Good Heaven! cried Don Quixote, what fooleries art thou stringing together, Sancho! pray, what relation have these old saws to the subject of our conversation?...." (1,25)

And:

Sancho said he might take his own way; tho' he himself should be glad to dispatch the business now he was warm, and while the mill was a-going; for, "Delay breeds danger;

and we ought still to be doing while to God we are sueing; I will give thee, is good; but, Here take it, is better: A sparrow in hand is worth an eagle on the wing." "No more proverbs, Sancho, for the love of God! cried the knight.... (2,71)

5) The Arcadian or pastoral theme. This was another of the popular genres of the time and a favourite of Cervantes, a kind of early romantic glance backward to a legendary rural world of peace, plenty and poetry. The theme starts up early in the novel as soon as Quixote stumbles upon a shepherds' camp and begins speechifying about the Golden Age. A shepherd's life is really rather lonesome and grotty, but all Cervantes' shepherds seem to sit around in camp with other shepherds singing songs and spouting poetry instead of fending off wolves, worms and hoof-rot. They also seem to enjoy rivetting love lives (for lonely shepherds). They have more in common with the inhabitants of Shakespeare's Forest of Arden than real shepherds just as Quixote's knights-errant have very little in common with the real-life thuggish mercenaries on horseback one encounters in medieval history.

There are a lot of shepherds (and some goatherds, not to mention runaway men and women dressed up as shepherds) in the first part of the novel especially in the Sierra Morena sequence. But the theme really blossoms near the end of the second part (2,58) when Quixote runs into a group of "people of fortune and fashion" who have come to the forest to dress up like swains and shepherdesses and "form a new pastoral Arcadia" based on poems they have read by Garcilaso and Camoens. This obviously repeats the pattern of Quixote's own story, the reading and imitation of genre fiction. Note also how Cervantes' Spain seems absolutely chock full of financially comfortable dilettante readers imitating the books they have read. It comes to mind that this episode constitutes an implicit critique of Quixote's own project and foreshadows his own return to sanity and rejection of knight-errantry at the end of the novel. It stands to reason that one of these air-headed proto-hippie shepherdesses has read Volume 1 of *Don Quixote* "from end to end" and gushes over the old knight in the mellifluous pseudo-archaic tones of romantic fiction.

"O my dear companion! cried she, what an happy accident
is this! that there knight, I assure thee, is the most valiant,
enamoured, and courteous person in the whole world...."

Shortly after spending an idyllic hour with these well-dressed
shepherdesses (think: Gore-Tex and microfibre), Quixote rides out
and is immediately crushed under a stampeding herd of bulls (so
much for glory, says Cervantes).

Later in the novel, after his defeat by the Knight of the White
Moon and his vow to abandon knight-errantry for a period of two
years, a disappointed Quixote happens to return to this spot.
Briefly, a new fancy burgeons in his manic brain and threatens to
hijack the book.

"This is the meadow, he said, where we met the gay
shepherdesses and gallant swains, who sought to renew and
react the pastoral Arcadia, a project equally original and
ingenious, in imitation of which, shouldst thou approve of
the scheme, I am resolved to assume the garb and employment of a shepherd during the term of my retirement. I
will purchase some sheep, together with all the necessary
implements of a pastoral life, and taking the name of
Quixotiz, while thou shalt bear that of the swain Pancino;
we shall stroll about through mountains, woods and mead-
ows, singing here, lamenting there...." (2,67)

A couple of pages later Quixote is run over by a stampeding herd of
hogs! (If you think Cervantes didn't intend to nail the parallel, you
have no idea how a writer's mind works.) Then he proceeds homeward to die, though before his final illness (and return to sanity) he
tries one more time to enlist his friends in this new pastoral project,
which he seems to view as an interim activity while he waits to
return to knight-errantry (2,73).

Cervantes himself wrote pastoral romances (for example, *Galatea*,
actually mentioned in *Don Quixote*). But for the purposes of this
novel, he suppresses his own preference and treats the genre satirical-
ly, in parallel (another transposition in a different key) with chivalric
romances. Both genres, according to the novel, inspire silly people to
perform especially silly acts. It's obvious that neither genre actually
suffered by being made fun of. My sons read contemporary Arthur-

ian romances by the bagfull (that whole fantasy-sci-fi-historical-romance publishing/marketing niche), and the pastoral (via Rousseau) threaded its way into contemporary treatments of native cultures (remember *Dances with Wolves*), the old cowboy stories, political correctness, vegetarianism, the national park system and Gore-Tex.

6) Topical reference. Think of Jane Austen. Her novels seem to be about a very narrowly defined world of young gentry (and their poor relatives) in drawing-rooms and country manses. Then you look more carefully at, say, *Mansfield Park*, and you notice that part of the reason the Bertram family falls apart is that the family's life of wealth and ease is built on slave-worked plantations in the colonies. The family's security begins to totter when something goes wrong with the plantation—it's never said in the novel, but clearly this relates to the British government's decision to outlaw slavery. Sir Thomas has to leave home for an extended period to repair matters. Chaos ensues.

Likewise in *Don Quixote* some such contextual referent stands behind the novel, only here and there filtering to the surface of the text. Spain's Moorish past is ever present in the person of the story's main narrator, Cid Hamet Benengeli, who once lived in la Mancha (where does he live now? one wonders; where did he go?) and writes in Arabic. Cervantes is repeating an historical message loop, whether he is conscious of it or not. The great Arabic libraries in Toledo and elsewhere on the peninsula were the main sources for the reintroduction of Greek and Roman texts into Europe after the Dark Ages. Eager translators followed on the heels of the Christian knights of the *reconquista*. So this is not the first time an old European tale has been routed through the Arab language.

I have already mentioned the two inset stories dealing with Moors. One tells of an escaped captive and his lover. ("In her body and dress, replied the stranger, she is a Moor, but altogether a christian in her soul; for, she longs ardently to be a professed convert to our faith." (1,37) No doubt the politically correct sentiment in the time and circumstances.) The second is rather more interesting and comes in two segments toward the end of the novel. In Volume 2, Chapter 54, Sancho encounters a band of German pilgrim-mummers, one of whom turns out to be a man named Ricote, a Morisco (Christianized Moor) shopkeeper in their home village. Ricote tells a story of growing certainty that he and his family would be expelled from Spain and, not wanting to end up in Africa, he left home to find some more suitable haven. Germany turned out to be the place, and now he has returned in disguise (as a pilgrim) to collect his buried fortune and find his family, which has in fact already been expelled. The story continues in Chapter 63 when Quixote and Sancho are present at the boarding of a Turkish brigantine. Ricote's lost daughter and her boyfriend just happen to be disguised among the crew. Ricote, too, just happens to be on hand —all this is evidence of a certain haste on the author's part and we needn't waste time on it (except to note its structural parallel with the Moorish captive story in Volume 1).

But the first part of the story is quite different in tone and detail; it has the feel of something real, not the conventional soap opera air of the inset stories. This strangeness, with its scent of reality and, yes, modernity, begins with the peculiar and precise details of these "outlandish" beggars, their staves and robes, their incomprehensible songs and cries for "Guelte" and continues with Ricote's amazing insider account of Renaissance ethnic cleansing. Here is the story as Ricote tells it ("in pure Castilian," as the narrator emphasizes):

"Well thou knowest, O Sancho Panza, my neighbour, and friend, how the edict, and proclamation, which his majesty published against those of my religion, overwhelmed us all with terror and consternation; at least, they terrified me to such a degree, that long before the time allotted to us for our removal from Spain, I thought the rigour of the penalty was already executed against me and my children. I therefore resolved, and I think, wisely, like the man who knowing he must quit the house he lives in, at such a time, provides himself with another to which he may remove—I resolved, I say, to retire by myself, without my family, and go in quest of some place to which I might carry it commodiously, without that hurry and confusion which attended the departure of my neighbours; for, I was very well convinced, and so were all our elders, that those edicts were not only threats, as some people said, but real laws, that would certainly be put in execution at the appointed time: and this truth I was compelled to believe, by knowing the base and mad designs which our people harboured; such designs that, I verily think, his majesty was divinely inspired to execute such a gallant resolution. Not that we were all guilty; for, some, among us, were firm, and staunch christians: but, they were few in number, that they could not oppose the schemes of those who were otherwise; and it was dangerous to nurse a serpent in one's bosom, by allowing the enemy to live within the house. In a word, we were justly chastized by the sentence of banishment, mild and gentle in the opinion of some, but to us the most terrible that could be pronounced. In what country soever we are, we lament our exile from Spain: for, in fine, here we were born; this is out native country; in no clime do we find a reception suitable to our misfortunes: nay, in Barbary, and all other parts of Africa, where we expected to be received, cherished, and entertained, we have been most injured and maltreated: we knew not our happiness until we lost it; and so intense is the longing desire which almost all of us have to return to Spain, that the greatest part of those, and they are many, who understand the language like me, return to this kingdom, leaving their wives, and children, unprotected abroad, such is their affection for this their native soil: and now, I know, by experience, the truth of the common saying, Sweet is the love of native land.

"Leaving our town, as I have already said, I repaired to France; and, tho' there we met with a civil reception, I was desirous of seeing other countries. I, therefore, travelled into Italy, from thence I passed into Germany, where people seemed to live with more freedom: the natives do not pry with curious eyes into one another's concerns; every one lives according to his own humour: for, in most parts of the empire there is liberty of conscience. I left a house which I hired in a village near Augsburg, and joined these pilgrims, a great number of whom are wont to come hither yearly, on pretence of visiting the sanctuaries of Spain, which are their Indies, as being productive of well known advantage, and most certain gain. They traverse the whole country; and there is not a village from which they are not dismissed with a belly full of meat and drink, as the saying is, and a rial, at least, in money; so that, at the end of their peregrination, they are above an hundred crowns in pocket, which, being changed into gold, they conceal in the hollow of their staves or in the patches of their cloaks, or task their industry in such a manner as to carry off their purchase to their own country, in spite of the guards at the passes and gates, where they are examined and registered.

"My present intention, Sancho, is to carry off the money I have buried, which, being without the town, I can retrieve without danger: then I shall write, or take passage from Valencia, to my wife and daughter, who, I know, are at Algiers, in order to contrive a method for transporting them to some port in France, from whence I will conduct them to Germany, where we will bear with resignation the will of heaven: for, in fine, Sancho, I am positively certain that my daughter Ricota, and my wife Francisca Ricote are real catholic christians: and, tho' I myself am not entirely of that way of thinking, I have more of the christian than the mussulman; and I incessantly pray to God to open the eyes of my understanding...." (2,54)

None of this account fits with the themes and structures of the novel as a whole (in the follow-up a few chapters later, we get the story of Ricota, his daughter, which conforms—desperate lovers, cross-dressing—more closely to the general pattern of the inset stories elsewhere). And Ricote's psychology, right down to his accurate description of mass denial and that confused assent-of-the-victim-to-judgment moment we have read about in accounts of Jews awaiting deportation in Nazi Europe, is so familiar and contemporary that one can't help thinking this is a story Cervantes heard or the voice of a man he actually knew. The economics of the story are fascinating as well, the way mid-Europe saw gold-rich Spain as "their Indies," the place to go and plunder for gold (just as now Moroccans and Turks flood into modern France and Germany for jobs). And having read this, one wonders exactly how Cervantes viewed his country's ethnic policies, what he thought of the Jews and the Arabs. What we have here is only a hint, though the rigorous focus, the attention to detail and the absence of irony suggest more than superficial sympathy.

Jews are mentioned in the novel only once. In Volume 2, Chapter 8, Sancho is babbling away to Quixote about why he thinks he should be written up in a book, the main reason being that he believes in God and the teachings of the Roman Catholic Church and is "a mortal enemy to Jews." And speaking of slavery and political correctness, it's fascinating to see Sancho eager to set himself up a slave exporter, as so many others did at the time, the moment he gets a chance. This occurs during the Dorotea-Princess Micomicona hoax when Sancho is promised a governorship in the princess' African homeland.

> ...and he said within himself, "Suppose my vassals are negroes, what else have I to do, but transport them to Spain, where I can sell them for ready money, with which I may purchase some title or post that will maintain me...all the days of my life!" (1,29)

No superego here. Sancho is utterly and irredeemably himself in such speeches. Betrayed by his mouth, he reveals himself as an unreconstructed Archie Bunker de la Mancha. All the more wonder that when he actually comes to governing an "island" late in the novel, his actions are measured, wise and honest. In Sancho's case the old saw runs backwards: it's not power that corrupts; it's lack of power. When he's given responsibility, he grows in stature, becomes his better self.

Other references seem more or less incidental though they still help to fill in the textural background of the novel. A character in one of the inset stories is off to be a judge on the Supreme Court of Mexico. Someone has a brother in Peru. In his speech on fame, Quixote mentions the "courteous Cortez" who burned his ships to keep his men from sailing back to Spain. Books and authors are mentioned numerous times; some of the literary discussions seem meant as backhand references to contemporary playwrights (Cervantes felt he was in competition with Lope de Vega who was immensely popular at the time). I have no evidence whatsoever for my intuition that the Duke and Duchess in Volume 2 are meant to stand for the new rich, flush with the inflated largesse of bullion from America (they just act like that).

84

DON QUIXOTE AND NOVEL FORM

*There was in Sevil, a certain madman, seized with the most diverting whim
that ever entered the brain of a lunatic. He used to walk with a hollow
cane, pointed at one end; and whenever he met with a dog in the street,
or in any other place, he clapped his foot on one of the creature's hind legs,
pulled up the other with his hand, and applying, as well as he could,
the pipe to his posteriors, instantly blew him up as round as a ball:
this operation being performed, he clapt him twice on the belly, and
dismissed the patient, saying, very bravely to the mob, that never failed
to gather round him, "Gentlemen, I suppose now, you think it is an
easy matter to blow up a dog." In a like manner, I say, "I suppose
your worship thinks it an easy matter to write a book."* (2,Preface)

Critics in Disarray

One can quickly become confused, bemused and befuddled reading the file on *Don Quixote*. Walter Starkie, in the introduction to his translation, writes, "Out of a spirit of *fin de siècle* melancholy sprang *Don Quixote*, the first modern novel in the world...." Harold Bloom, in *How to Read and Why*, calls it "the first and best of all novels, which nevertheless is more than a novel...." In the *New York Times*, Carlos Fuentes writes, "If for many reasons *Don Quixote* is the first modern novel, it is pre-eminently because...." Walter Benjamin called it "the earliest perfect specimen of the novel."

But other critics tell us that it's not the first novel or not even a novel at all. Ian Watt, in *The Rise of the Novel*, begins the history of the novel with Defoe's *Robinson Crusoe* in England in the early eighteenth century because it reflects the common-sense realism of the rising English middle class. André Malraux said Madame de Lafayette's *La Princesse de Clèves* (1678) was the first novel because it concentrates on depicting the inner emotional life of a character. In *From Dawn to Decadence*, Jacques Barzun gives credit for inventing the new genre to the anonymous author of *La Vida de Lazarillo de Tormes* (1554).

> What makes the work, though short, a true novel is this double subject: character and social scene, both treated matter-of-factly and by inference critically. *Don Quixote* does indeed contain elements of what is the distinctive subject matter of the novel, but it merges them with allegory and philosophy. It is not bound by the plausible, whereas the novel pretends to be genuine history, full of real people and places. (*From Dawn to Decadence*, 111)

It's actually not so difficult to figure out what the problem is here. When you look at what critics say about the novel, you find roughly five schools of thought; let's call them the strict realist, the hybrid, the weak thematic, the easy-going (romantic and postmodern) and the experimental. The problem then is that no-one actually ever tells you there are five schools of thought. The poor reader or the neophyte novelist assumes everyone is on the same map when the subject of novels comes up when, in fact, there are multiple maps and they're not congruent. They have fallen into what Milan Kundera calls "the slough where everyone thinks he understands everything without understanding anything."

The primary cleavage upon which theories of the novel divide is the concept of reality. Most theories are deficient because they privilege one type of novel, a particular era, a social class, or a particular subject matter: reality, the plausible, or as Theodor Adorno calls it "mere existence" (where the idea of what constitutes reality tends toward a capitalist bourgeois common sense definition of the term). With or without being conscious of it, every novelist begins by making quite complicated decisions about what is and is not realistic. In a sense, every novel moves the goalposts this way or that; every novel puts into question the nature of reality.

If you define plausibility strictly in terms of contemporary, common sense, everyday reality, then all sorts of texts and textual moves become non-novelistic. Old-fashioned motifs, borrowed from romance, epic and myth, become non-novelistic. Certain forms, such as the allegory, which direct the reader to a reality beyond the surface reality of the text, become non-novelistic. Form itself, the aesthetic exfoliation of repetitions, doubles and reflecting parallels, becomes non-novelistic. And anything that draws attention in the text to the fact that you are reading a book is non-novelistic. This last item involves a paradox: a novel assumes a certain definition of reality, but if that definition becomes an explicit part of the text the text becomes unrealistic. In other words, if the novel becomes too aware of itself as a novel, it somehow ceases to be a novel at all.

Don Quixote is exuberantly and self-consciously problematic on every single one of these points, which, in turn, problematizes much modern critical thought about novels. In fact, it's possible to read Cervantes' attack on those false, misleading and dishonest chivalric romances as an attack on verisimilitude, the suspension of disbelief, and books that pretend to seduce us into thinking they are true. Cervantes moves the goalposts to include the book itself; a book that does not confess its own bookishness as part of its reality is a fraud. Of course, this is partly a very witty joke, a play on the paradox of verisimilitude, the quality of *seeming* to be real. From the outset, Cervantes engages with the fakery of his own project; he composes that odd thing, an anti-novel, a book against books.

Or, to put this another way, Cervantes composes out of an

awareness of the various novelistic possibilities suggested by the multiple meanings of that word "reality." At the outset, he invents a new form, playfully aware of itself as a book. But the history of the novel took another path, the path of verisimilitude. Writing about Laurence Sterne's *Tristram Shandy* and Denis Diderot's *Jacques le Fataliste*, similarly bookish books, Kundera makes a parallel argument.

> They reach heights of playfulness, of lightness, never scaled before or since. Afterward, the novel got itself tied to the imperative of verisimilitude, to realistic settings, to chronological order. It abandoned the possibilities opened up by these two masterpieces, which could have led to a different development of the novel (yes, it's possible to imagine a whole other history of the European novel....) (*The Art of the Novel*, 15)

As a matter of fact, however, it actually seems as if the novel followed several historical trajectories at once. While one kind of novel followed the path of conventional realism, what we might call an alternative tradition of self-consciousness, complexity, experiment, elaboration and playfulness has flourished simultaneously, though perhaps with leaner commercial success.

The Strict Realists

Strict critics tend to believe in progress, that one form develops out of another and is appropriate to its place and time. Hence romance follows myth (or epic) and novel follows romance. When the word "novel" was first used in its present sense becomes important in this argument. (Some romantic souls, putting a premium on orality and myth, view this line of development as a decline instead of progress; Mircea Eliade called the nineteenth-century novel "the great repository of degraded myths.") Ian Watt, for example, in *The Rise of the Novel*, ties the emergence of the novel in eighteenth-century England to the development of a new book-buying middle-class audience, which put a value on common sense, contemporary situations and fictional characters much like themselves. Thus strict realists tend to define the novel in terms of its subject matter and treatment, that is, novels are about recognizably real people in real-life situations. And the word "recognizably" here refers to modern consumer-readers.

> With the help of their larger perspective the historians of the novel have been able to do much more to determine the idiosyncratic features of the new form. Briefly, they have seen 'realism' as the defining characteristic which differentiates the work of the early eighteenth-century novelists from previous fiction. (Ian Watt, *The Rise of the Novel*, 10)

Novels are about people like us, by which I mean a broad coalition of decently educated readers of no fixed ethnic or national address—as opposed to gods, goddesses, talking animals, magical beings, towering heroes and palpitating heroines. Allegories, in which characters stand for something outside the narrative, also don't count as novels. Science fiction, fantasy and even detective novels are romances. I even recall a reviewer in the *New York Review of Books* claiming that William Gass' novel *The Tunnel* wasn't actually a novel—presumably it had gone over some experimental edge into chaos.

Strict realist critics, like Watt and Barzun, don't consider *Don Quixote* a novel because of its improbable characters and its uncomfortable proximity to the romance (with its kings, queens, knights-errant, damsels in distress, mystical loves, magic potions, giants, dragons). The quality of its realism is suspect. As Nabokov observes, "...the picture Cervantes paints of the country is about as true and typical of seventeenth-century Spain as Santa Claus is true and typical of the twentieth-century North Pole." (*Lectures on Don Quixote*, 4) But then Nabokov also says we should never look for reality in novels anyway.

A stronger case can be made for the strict realist position if we drop the word "real" and substitute words like "plausibility" or "verisimilitude." In a sense, one can see the development of myth to romance to novel as linked to the evolution of the human idea of plausibility. As Walter Benjamin points out in his essay "The Storyteller," the rise of the novel coincides with a new use of language, the communication of information. Information (fact) is characterized by its verifiability. Once upon a time, people thought stories of gods, goddesses and heroes were perfectly plausible, their truth was backed by the authority of the speaker, the storyteller himself, whereas in the information age, the criterion of plausibility has changed.

But nevertheless the strict realist school comes with a number of problems attached not the least of which is that it generates endless and embarrassing debates over what's in and what's out. These debates often ride on the meaning of that slippery word "reality" and how it gets positioned in the novel in question. The level of discussion can become awfully nitpicking. Can a novel be too stylish to be realistic?

> In France, the classical critical outlook, with its emphasis on elegance and concision, was not fully challenged until the coming of Romanticism. It is perhaps partly for this reason that French fiction from *La Princesse de Clèves* to *Les Liaisons dangereuses* stands outside the main tradition of the novel. For all its psychological penetration and literary skill, we feel it is too stylish to be authentic. (*The Rise of the Novel*, 30)

And these in turn give rise to even stranger debates about the relative purity of any particular instance of a novel or novel-like piece of fiction. Does it suffer a taint of allegory? Of romance? Are there too many essay-like digressions? Too many interpolated stories? Does it also draw attention to itself as a book, making mock of verisimilitude and those who read for it? All these are aspects of works we often want to call novels (for example, *Don Quixote*) but which don't fit the definition. So that out of the strict theory is born what I call the hybrid theory of the novel, the novel as the mongrel offspring of the epic and the printing press (or some other unholy act of miscegenation). "The forms of prose fiction are mixed," says Northrop Frye, in *The Anatomy of Criticism*, "like racial strains in human beings, not separable like the sexes." (305)

The Hybrid School

Frye, the best example of a complex hybridist, called *Don Quixote*
"the world's first and perhaps still its greatest novel." (*Canadian
Forum,* 1949) Frye's awareness of the ining and outing problem of
the strict theory (which he classifies as "low mimetic") drives his
thinking about novel form. "The usual critical approach," he writes,
"to the form of such works resembles that of the doctors in Brob-
dingnag, who after great wrangling finally pronounced Gulliver a
lusus naturae." (*Anatomy,* 313) For example:

> ...we recognize that *The Marble Faun* is not a typical low
> mimetic fiction: it is dominated by an interest that looks
> back to fictional romance and forward to the ironic mythi-
> cal writers of the next century—to Kafka, for instance, or
> Cocteau. This interest is often called allegory, but probably
> Hawthorne himself was right in calling it romance. We can
> see how this interest tends toward abstraction in character-
> drawing, and if we know no other canons than low mimetic
> ones, we complain of this. (*The Anatomy of Criticism,* 137-
> 138)

To solve the ining and outing problem, Frye teases apart the
romance (mid-way between myth and novel), the novel (realistic),
the confession or autobiography and the anatomy or Menippean
satire (the encyclopedic narrative trajectory) and shows how these
distinct forms are often mixed.

> The six possible combinations of all these forms all exist,
> and we have shown how the novel has combined with each
> of the other three. Exclusive concentration on one form is
> rare: the early novels of George Eliot, for instances, are
> influenced by the romance, and the later ones by the
> anatomy. The romance-confession hybrid is found, natu-
> rally, in the autobiography of a romantic temperament, and
> is represented in English by the extroverted George Borrow
> and the introverted De Quincy. The romance-anatomy one
> we have noticed in Rabelais; the later example is *Moby
> Dick,* where the romantic theme of the wild hunt expands

into an encyclopaedic anatomy of the whale. Confession and anatomy are united in *Sartor Resartus* and in some of Kierkegaard's strikingly original experiments in prose fiction form, including *Either/Or*. More comprehensive fictional schemes usually employ at least three forms: we can see strains of the novel, romance and confession in *Pamela*, or novel, romance and anatomy in *Don Quixote*, of novel, confession and anatomy in Proust, and of romance, confession and anatomy in Apuleius. (*The Anatomy of Criticism*, 312-313)

I checked the math, and of course there are not just six but 24 possible combinations of romance, novel, confession and anatomy, or eight if we only consider combinations of the novel with the other three genres. What happened to the other eighteen (or two) in Frye's view, I have no idea. But this admittedly schematic approach does have the advantage of being less judgmental and Procrustean when it comes to reading actual works of fiction than the strict method. Though one begins to wonder if there is any such animal as a novel strictly defined, save, perhaps, for *Moll Flanders* and *Robinson Crusoe*, which provide Watt with his template of novel form.

Frye's archetypal criticism does acknowledge the realistic tendency of the novel, but fits the novel into a grid of identities and gradations so that any work exists in a state of tension between its mythic archetype or form and what is more humanly plausible to our contemporary senses. "In myth," Frye writes, "we see the structural principles of literature isolated; in realism we see the *same* structural principles (not similar ones) fitting into a context of plausibility." (*Anatomy of Criticism*, 136) In other words, the central core or form of a piece of fiction (its plot) is actually what Frye calls "antirepresentational," that is, unrealistic, insofar as it reflects the conventionalized structure of myth.

It is clear that the novel was a realistic displacement of romance, and had few structural features peculiar to itself. *Robinson Crusoe, Pamela, Tom Jones*, use much the same general structure as romance, but adapt the structure to a demand for greater conformity to ordinary experience. (*The Secular Scripture, A Study of the Structure of Romance*, 38-39)

The thing to notice about this position, as our analysis proceeds, is Frye's passing remark that the novel has "few structural features peculiar to itself." The word "structure" here is interchangeable with the word "form." And what he is saying is that the characteristics we associate with the novel (realism, verisimilitude, plausibility) are not characteristics of form. The form or structure of a novel is borrowed from the romance, which in turn borrows its form from larger "structural principles of literature" which are grounded in mythic archetypes. Thus, unlike the strict realists, Frye posits an actual form for the novel; it's just not a form that is specific to the novel alone.

The Weak Thematic

The weak thematic school of novel theory sides with Watt and Frye in defining the essential nature of the novel as realistic but frames the argument differently by placing its emphasis on theme instead of treatment. These critics look at *Don Quixote* and read the old don's disillusionment as a watershed in literary history, the moment when the romance, the fantasies of myth and epic, finally capitulate before the (doubtful) splendour of common sense. These critics are still wedded to the idea of the strict connection between the novel form and realism, but they cheat just a tiny bit, allowing that while *Don Quixote* is not exactly realistic itself, its theme is the discovery of reality behind the haze of legendary appearances. On this reading, *Don Quixote* is a sort of parable of the birth of the novel, the birth of the modern. Quixote stands for fantasy; Sancho stands for earthy realism.

These weak thematic critics are the ones most likely to call *Don Quixote* the first novel, or the first modern novel. And to a certain extent their view has become the prevailing one amongst people who haven't read or thought about the book very much. In his essay "Manners, Morals, and the Novel" Lionel Trilling famously enunciated the received wisdom:

In any genre it may happen that the first great example contains the whole potentiality of the genre. It has been said that all philosophy is a footnote to Plato. It can be said that all prose fiction is a variation on the theme of *Don Quixote*. Cervantes sets for the novel the problem of appearance and reality: the shifting and conflict of social classes becomes the field of the problem of knowledge, of how we know and how reliable our knowledge is, which at that very moment of history is vexing the philosophers and scientists. (Trilling, *The Moral Obligation to be Intelligent*, 108)

Trilling, of course, is not to blame, but this quotation, at least the part that reads "...all prose fiction is a variation on the theme of *Don Quixote*" has become a critical cliché, the usual opening for a run-of-the mill review of any new translation and the standard bookseller's blurb (do a quick web search and you'll find it on dozens of sites). And the trouble with clichés is that they are often true but in a trivial way. Yes, it seems to be the case that at some level most novels involve someone distinguishing appearance from reality. All stories, too. Most thought—all of science—is about appearance and reality. But in what way does the theme distinguish a novel from anything else?

The difference, as I say, between the strict realist and weak thematic critics lies in the way they position the word "reality" in the context of so-called novel form. Strict critics require realistic characters, realistic settings, plausible story lines, and everyday situations. The weak thematic critics relax their standards somewhat in terms of the manner of the telling while requiring that the theme of the novel present a progression from appearance to reality. This line of thought leads to another commonplace of novel theory, that all novels are *bildungsromans*, novels of education.

Like any narrative form, the novel has a typical action, with thematic value, which is peculiarly its own.

The matter of the novel—the theme that has informed the genre from *Don Quixote* onward—is relatively uncomplicated. The novel records the passage from a state of innocence to a state of experience, from that ignorance which is bliss to a mature recognition of the actual way

94

of the world. In the less loaded terms of Lionel Trilling, the novel deals with a distinction between appearance and reality. It is not necessarily a question of ontological subtleties: the reality to which the novel appeals is that to which it is historically connected, the reality of bourgeois life, of business, and of the modern city. (Maurice Z. Shroder, "The Novel as a Genre," *The Theory of the Novel*, Stevick, Ed., 14)

And somehow, in the popular mind, this appearance versus reality argument meshes with the equally ubiquitous romantic perception of Quixote as one of the most gloriously alive characters in literature (Bloom will keep nattering on about Quixote and Falstaff as if the two had something in common). Sentimental readers value the old don's defiance in the face of humdrum reality (the dream-the-impossible-dream school of criticism), his madly romantic project of re-establishing knight-errantry in an unromantic age. My God! He gets to say things like:

> "Know, friend Sancho, that I was born by heaven's appointment, in these iron times, to revive the age of gold, or the golden age! I am he, for whom strange perils, valiant deeds, and vast adventures are reserved." (1,20)

But there are problems, if not outright contradictions, inherent in this view. If the novel is about the defeat of fantasy by realism, then Quixote is a sad, pathetic depressive on a manic tear. It's a novel of disillusionment, which is why Dostoevsky called it the saddest book ever written. If the novel is about the human spirit persevering in the face of harsh reality, then the fact that Quixote himself renounces knight-errantry at the end of the novel is a deeply puzzling contradiction. What was the author thinking? (One realizes, of course, that the popular mind has never been strong on thinking things through.)

The Easy-Going (Romantic)

Early in *The Rise of the Novel*, Watt makes a fascinating admission. Having refined his definition by adding the proposition that the novel conceives itself in terms of rejecting all models, especially traditional literary models and traditional plots, he blurts out the odd fact that there isn't much left; the novel in the strict sense is a formless form.

> On the other hand, it is surely damaging for a novel to be in any sense an imitation of another literary work: and the reason for this seems to be that since the novelist's primary task is to convey the impression of fidelity to human experience, attention to any pre-established formal conventions can only endanger his success. What is often felt as the formlessness of the novel, as compared, say, with tragedy or the ode, probably follows from this: the poverty of the novel's formal conventions would seem to be the price it must pay for its realism. (13)

In other words, Watt's definition of a novel self-destructs; it unwrites itself as he writes it. Or it becomes the definition of a content without a form. Hence, the logical problem for all strict, not-quite-so-strict and hybrid critics becomes: What is a formless form, a form that seems only to exist in concrete instances as a hybrid of other forms? Doesn't this question leave open the possibility that there is a way of thinking about the novel that is inclusive rather than exclusive, in which all these so-called "forms" mixed together make some organic or formal sense on their own?

The Russian critic Mikhail Bakhtin, from the Romantic wing of what I call the easy-going school of novel theory, offers a delightfully witty solution to this riddle. He simply flips the problem of the amorphous nature of the novel into a definition of the novel: the form of the novel is an organized structure of multiple genres and discourses which reflects the fundamental heteroglossia of language itself.

> The novel [writes Bakhtin] can be defined as a diversity of social speech types (sometimes even a diversity of lan-

guages) and a diversity of individual voices, artistically organized.... Authorial speech, the speeches of narrators, inserted genres, the speech of characters are merely those fundamental compositional unities with whose help heteroglossia can enter the novel; each of them permits a multiplicity of social voices and a wide variety of their links and interrelationships (always more or less dialogized). These distinctive links and interrelationships between utterances and languages, this movement of the theme through different languages and speech types, its dispersion into the rivulets and droplets of social heteroglossia, its dialogization—this is the basic distinguishing feature of the stylistics of the novel.

In other words, the novel is the genre above all genres because it reflects the fundamental conflicted multiform nature of language itself—the way language as a whole splits up into competing discourses or sub-languages. Bakhtin calls *Don Quixote* "the classic and purest model of the novel as a genre...which realizes in itself, in extraordinary depth and breadth, all the artistic possibilities of heteroglot and internally dialogized novelistic discourse." (*The Dialogic Imagination*, 324) But he discovers novels as far back as ancient Greece, including works by such authors as Xenophon, Achilles Tatius and Chariton, as well as the better known Menippus, Lucian and Petronius, and, closer to us, Rabelais, none of which find their way into lists of what we normally think of as novels. In particular, he mentions a novel called *An Ethiopian Tale* or *Aethiopica* which is especially interesting in the present context:

> ...the longest—and by many considered to be the best—of the still extant Greek novels, or *erotika pathemata* (tales of suffering from love). The author, Heliodorus (fl. 220-250 A.D.)...was heavily influenced by the cult of Helios. The novel was exceptionally influential even in modern times: Scaliger and Tasso admired him; Calderon (*Los Hijos de la fortuna*) and Cervantes (the unfortunate *Persiles y Sigismunda*) imitated it. (*The Dialogic Imagination*, 86n.)

I call Bakhtin's position the Romantic wing of the easy-going school because it has a kind of romantic panache (he sees the novel as by definition comic and subversive, a battle of discourses as a counterpoint to the one discourse of authority) but also because he seems to have borrowed it from the eighteenth-century German Romantics (not romantic in the small-r sentimental sense, not related to the romance as a literary genre), specifically the Schlegel brothers, Friedrich and August Wilhelm. In a lecture in 1789, August Wilhelm, the older brother, called *Don Quixote* a "perfect masterwork of higher romantic art." (Quoted in "Romanticism in Literature" by René Wellek in *Dictionary of the History of Ideas*, Vol 4, 188.) And in a book called *Kritisch Ausgabe,* Friedrich wrote:

> The idea of a novel, as it is established by Boccaccio and Cervantes, is the idea of a romantic book, a romantic composition, where all the forms and all the genres are mixed and interwoven. In the novel, the principal mass is furnished by prose, more diverse than that of any genre set by the Ancients. There are historical parts, rhetorical parts, parts in dialogue; all these styles alternate, they are interwoven and related in the most ingenious and the most artificial way. Poems in all genres, lyrical, epic, didactic, as well as romances, are scattered throughout the whole and embellish it in a varied and exuberant profusion and diversity in the richest and most brilliant fashion. The novel is a poem of poems, a whole texture of poems. It is obvious that a poetic composition of this kind, produced from such varied elements and forms where external conditions are not strictly limited, allows a much more artificial poetic interweaving than the epic or drama, insofar as the first requires a unity of tone while the second must be easily summed up and apprehended, since it is to be offered to the intuition. (Quoted in Tzetvan Todorov's *Mikhail Bakhtin, The Dialogic Principle*, 86)

Of course, the question arises as to how what Bakhtin calls heteroglossia distinguishes the novel from anything else. And when he tries to contrast the novel with its predecessor, the epic, his argument first becomes murky (he calls the novel "a genre-in-the-making" and "this most fluid of genres" and "a genre without a canon") and then begins to consolidate his definition around a second set of co-ordinates that sound an awful lot like Ian Watt infected by Hegel.

> I find three characteristics that fundamentally distinguish
> the novel in principle from other genres: (1) its stylistic
> three-dimensionality, which is linked with the multi-
> languaged consciousness realized in the novel; (2) the radi-
> cal change it effects in the temporal co-ordinates of the
> literary image; (3) the new zone opened by the novel for
> structuring literary images, namely, the zone of maximal
> contact with the present (with contemporary reality) in all
> its open-endedness. (*The Dialogic Imagination*, 11)

The first distinguishing characteristic here refers to the aforementioned heteroglossia. And in Bakhtin's analysis, the second and
third distinguishing characteristics tend to amount to the same
thing, what Tzetvan Todorov calls "a single great opposition: possible or impossible continuity between the time of the (represen-
ted) utterance and the time of (representing) uttering." (*Mikhail
Bakhtin, The Dialogic Imagination*, 89) The epic is written as a representation of an "absolute past," a past, as Bakhtin says, that "is
walled off absolutely from all subsequent times" (*The Dialogic Imagination*, 15). Whereas

> To portray an event on the same time-and-value plane as
> oneself and one's contemporaries (and an event that is
> therefore based on personal experience and thought) is to
> undertake a radical revolution, and to step out of the world
> of epic into the world of the novel. (*The Dialogic Imagi-
> nation*, 14)

In effect, Bakhtin seems only to put a temporal spin on the conventional strict realist distinction between stories about gods, kings,
knights-errant, damsels-in-distress, dragons and giants and stories
that represent a world that seems more contemporary and real. And
he only adds to the ining and outing problem of the strict school by
saying things like:

> In the era of Hellenism a closer contact with the heroes of
> the Trojan epic cycle began to be felt; epic is already being
> transformed into novel. (*The Dialogic Imagination*, 15)

The Easy-Going (Postmodern)

Milan Kundera provides what might be called a postmodern variant of the easy-going school of novel theory. In an interview with Philip Roth in 1980, Kundera defined the novel as:

> a long piece of synthetic prose based on play with invented characters. These are the only limits. By the term synthetic I have in mind the novelist's desire to grasp his subject from all sides and in the fullest possible completeness. Ironic essay, novelistic narrative, autobiographical fragment, historic fact, flight of fantasy: The synthetic power of the novel is capable of combining everything into a unified whole like the voices of polyphonic music. The unity of a book need not stem from the plot, but can be provided by the theme.

This actually sounds a bit like Bakhtin; the words "polyphony" and "heteroglossia" seem superficially similar and both Bakhtin and Kundera like to use the works of Rabelais as an example of novel discourse. But where Bakhtin is a Romantic, Kundera is more of a hip Enlightenment rationalist; where Bakhtin finds the novel's roots in the parody of authoritative forms like the epic, Kundera finds them in the spirit of intellectual inquiry and playfulness of Cervantes, Diderot and Sterne (a completely different novel tradition, as I have said, than that cited by Watt and the strict realists); where Bakhtin defines the novel, in contrast with the epic, in terms of its temporal relationship to the present, Kundera allows it an almost illimitable freedom in terms of treatment and subject; and where Bakhtin inevitably edges toward the strict realists, Kundera emphasizes the possibility of different kinds of novels. (Interesting to notice how the Romantic tends toward the conservative and the rationalist tends toward the revolutionary.)

> ...the novel got itself tied to the imperative of verisimilitude, to realistic settings, to chronological order. It abandoned the possibilities opened by these two masterpieces [*Tristram Shandy* and *Jacques le Fataliste*], which could have led to a different development of the novel (yes, it's pos-

sible to imagine a whole other history of the European novel...). (*The Art of the Novel*, 15)

In an interview published in *The Art of the Novel*, Kundera talks about his book *The Book of Laughter and Forgetting*, which, as he points out, doesn't even have a single plot line but is, instead, held together by a pattern of repeated themes and motifs. "Is it a novel?" he asks. "Yes, to my mind. The novel is a meditation on existence as seen through the medium of imaginary characters." (*The Art of the Novel*, 83) This definition seems too broad for his interlocutor who asks if Kundera would consider *The Decameron* a novel. "All of its stories are connected by the same theme of love and told by the same ten narrators...." Kundera replies:

> I won't be so provocative as to call *The Decameron* a novel. Still, that book is one of the first efforts in modern Europe to create a large-scale composition in narrative prose, and as such it has a place in the history of the novel *at least* as its source and forerunner. You know, the novel took the particular historical path it took. It could just as easily have taken a completely different one. The novel form is almost boundless freedom. Throughout its history, the novel hasn't taken advantage of that. It has missed out on that freedom. It has left unexplored many formal possibilities. (*The Art of the Novel*, 83)

The reference here to "novel form" seems a bit disingenuous, if not completely contradictory, when linked with the words "boundless freedom." And Kundera never says why he wouldn't call *The Decameron* a novel. In *The Art of the Novel* he explores the analogy between musical composition (the idea of variations) and novel composition and spends a good deal of time mulling over how Hermann Broch somewhat clumsily inserted non-novel-like essays into his novel *The Sleepwalkers* (thus opening up new formal possibilities for the novel). He also includes an essay nominally about *Don Quixote* in which he says:

> Indeed, for me, the founder of the Modern Era is not only Descartes but also Cervantes.... If it is true that philosophy and science have forgotten about man's being, it emerges all the more plainly that with Cervantes a great European

art took shape that is nothing more than the investigation of this forgotten being. (*The Art of the Novel*, 4-5)

(Kundera's phrase "forgotten being" is a reference to Edmund Husserl's critique of modernity, but it seems eerily to echo the forgotten lore of knight-errantry and Eliade's "degraded myths.") But when it comes to novel form itself he remains maddeningly vague, preferring to emphasize the novel's open-ended and investigative aspects while sounding inspirational and occasionally a tad portentous.

> Indeed, it's important to understand what a novel is. A historian tells you about events that have taken place. By contrast, Raskolnikov's crime never saw the light of day. A novel examines not reality but existence. And existence is not what has occurred, existence is the realm of human possibilities, everything that man can become, everything he's capable of. Novelists draw up *the map of existence* by discovering this or that human possibility. (*The Art of the Novel*, 42)

This is a prolix way of reminding us that novels are imagined, made-up, fictional and, as such, aren't tied to actual events. It is Kundera's way of emphasizing one of his main points, the aim of freeing the novel from "the imperative of verisimilitude." By emphasizing the elements of playfulness, investigation, thought and dream over the demand for strict plausibility, Kundera is trying to provide a (still vague) theoretical underpinning for all those ironic late, high or postmodern concoctions which tend to break the strict realist mould, the return of the epic in Joyce, the return of the parable in Kafka, the polyhistoricism of the new historical novel, the re-introduction of oral consciousness in Third World novels, etc. And given the difficulties already demonstrated, it's no wonder that he can't seem to come up with a really concrete definition of a novel. Yet there is something appealingly quixotic about his non-definitions. A novel, he writes, "is often...nothing but a long quest for some elusive definitions." (*The Art of the Novel*, 127)

The Experimental Novel

We can imagine these various definitions of the novel as being on a continuum from right to left (without prejudice) and imagine each of the steps along the way as a steady displacement of the idea of realism in relation to the novel. Kundera is a writer who regards realism as an historical choice, a choice made among many options, and a choice that unnecessarily limited the development of novel form. (Notice the unstated assumption that form is somehow prior to and separate from the idea of novelistic realism.) The next logical position to the left of the easy-going school is the one that abandons the ideas of realism and plausibility completely.

Essentially, experimental novelists do what Bakhtin did and flip an aspect of the strict realist definition to make a new definition. The late American experimentalist John Hawkes once said that "plot, character, setting and theme" are the enemies of the novel, while "structure—verbal and psychological coherence—is still my largest concern as a writer. Related and corresponding event, recurring image and recurring action, these constitute the essential substance and meaningful density of writing." Generally speaking, plot, character, setting and theme are the structures that promote verisimilitude in a work of fiction, whereas repetitions, image patterns and subplots, the sorts of repetitions and correspondences Hawkes is referring to, while necessary in any work of art, tend to undermine verisimilitude. Such structures promote coherence, focus and symmetry in a way that insists on the bookishness of the work rather than concealing the author's guiding hand.

Experimental novelists intensify these aesthetic patterns or accentuate literary process and technique or invent anti-structures designed to destroy the structures of verisimilitude. For example, in his novel *The Bark Tree*, Raymond Queneau composes a plot linked entirely by coincidences. Or in Hubert Aquin's novels *Blackout* and *The Antiphonary*, events on the plot line are repeated just as in Hawkes' novel *The Lime Twig* an identical pair of birds hovers at the edge of two different but simultaneous scenes. Or Viktor Shklovsky uses a device he calls "baring the device" in which he tells the reader what literary device he is using and how it works. Character doubles, which are an intensification of the device of subplot, subvert the common sense notion of personal identity. Sometimes an experimental author will simply insert impossible "facts" as in *The Lime Twig* a horse named Rock Castle attains the advanced age of 54. Or they will reach for surreal associations or complex and counter-intuitive point-of-view structures.

What seems to be the case with experimental fiction is that it is always written with other, more conventional books or conventional notions of reality in mind; one of the primary effects of experimental work is the denial of expectation, the surprise the reader feels when form is inverted or twists back on itself or is in some other way subverted. Most commonly the experimental artist does this simply by drawing attention to the work of art as a work of art. A painting isn't about the image it represents; it's about surface, shape and colour. A book is a book. In this way, oddly enough, the experimental novel is tied to the strict realist novel, the same but opposite, like the right and left hand. They are both committed to a species of honesty, authenticity, or "realism." But the larger novel tradition swears allegiance to verisimilitude while the experimental tradition diminishes the importance of illusion and highlights the reality of the work itself, its materials, tools and process. The goalposts, as I say, have been moved.

In *Don Quixote* we find many of the experimental structures just mentioned carefully deployed along with devices now associated with what we call meta-fiction. It's a novel about books (and love). The explicit narrative motivation for the text is to ridicule and destroy the popular fictional genre known as chivalric romances, novels that are false and misleading because they pretend things like knights-errant, chaste damsels, giants and necromancers are real (they make them *seem* real). In Volume 2, the narrator explains how he has altered his structure in view of critical reviews of Volume 1. All the major characters in the second part of the novel have read Volume 1 (except for Quixote and Sancho themselves). Many have read a second book which purports to be a sequel, and somehow this spurious second part has spawned a man who wanders around Spain in armour calling himself Don Quixote (there is also a spurious Sancho Panza).

So far as I know no-one has called *Don Quixote* an experimental novel though, in fact, I'm not sure why. Perhaps it is the effect of a certain chronological arrogance, the assumption that what came earlier must be more primitive than what followed. We can call this the historical or evolutionary fallacy; the arrow of development only points one way. Some aspects of culture (science and technology) seem to work that way, but it's not clear that art always does. It's possible, I think, to make a case that two novels, *Don Quixote* and *Tristram Shandy*, displayed almost the full range of techniques in use today by novelists of whatever ilk.

The Form of Form

To summarize: the standard definitions of the novel often claim to be based on some idea of novel form, although in the end they are usually keyed, instead, to content (realistic) or theme or the treatment of time (a branch of the content argument). All these definitions seem to say something interesting about novels and the distinction between novels and other genres (epic, romance, short story), but they fail on the level of specificity. Either they are too exclusive or too inclusive. *Don Quixote* is and isn't a novel, the first novel, the most perfect novel. These definitions fail to be definitive.

Worse yet, by confusing form and content, they often distort our reading of any given novel. If we assume beforehand that the theme of a novel is appearance and reality, then we are less likely to notice when the novel is in fact about something else (and I use the word "about" here in the broadest possible sense). This seems to be the case with various readings and misreadings of *Don Quixote*.

In the end, realistic content doesn't turn out to be an entirely satisfactory criterion for deciding whether this or that book is a novel. In fact, it seems more like what Merlin Donald in his *The Origins of the Modern Mind* calls a "front-end" or tactical consideration, one of the options available to novels. What is missing is a more strategic (formal) idea of how a novel works. Northrop Frye's archetypal criticism is the one theory that endeavors to supply a strategic map. The form of a novel, he seems to say, like the form of the romance, is based on the structure of myths. In this view, a novel is fictional prose work that gives a more or less realistic treatment (character, setting, theme, motivation, etc.) of a mythic plot often in combination with other non-novelistic structures (anatomy, romance, etc.). But Frye's critical system begs another question. Why do myths and romances have the form they have? What is the form of form?

Put this another way: if we take all the preceding definitions together and agree that each of them supplies an observation about what a novel is, without actually being definitive, we come up with an interesting set of characteristics:

1) Novels are long. No-one among the critics considered here actually mentions this except Kundera. One thinks of E. M. Forster's terse and pragmatic definition: a novel is a "fictitious prose work over 50,000 words."

2) Novels are made up; they follow the actions of made-up characters.

3) But there is a marked trend among novels toward the plausible, that is, though they are made up, novels often seem to be about people and situations that could be real.

4) As soon as one says this, however, one has to backtrack and specify that the novel as a whole incorporates a counter-trend that is playful, ironic or experimental. What is plausible may be ignored, subverted, displaced or redefined within the novel itself.

5) Novels deploy a number of competing or contrasting discourses (polyglossia or heteroglossia), much as does language as a whole.

6) Novels are subversive in that by representing discourses in competition, by challenging, parodying, ridiculing discourses, they put at defiance the idea that there is a single authoritative discourse. There is a sense in which comedy and parody are native to the novel as a genre.

7) Novels often incorporate non-novelistic structures or devices such as aesthetic patterns (repetitions, subplots, image patterns), philosophy, essays, parables, myth-based plots, other genres (anatomy, romance, etc.) This point is a bit tricky because what is "non-novelistic" tends to be defined in terms of the strict realist novel. One would like to imagine a definition that would incorporate all those elements one actually does find in novels as part of the definition.

8) Novels have an interrogative, investigative, open-ended

quality; they map possible worlds, at least, worlds that are possible to describe in words.

9) Novels do not seem to have a form that is peculiar to themselves, rather novel form has evolved out of earlier forms. Many of the changes that have come about are front-end, tactical developments (for example, a preference for certain sorts of treatments, a trend toward a more contemporary vision of what is plausible, the ironizing of mythic elements, etc.).

Anything one might want to say about novels in general should probably have a list of characteristics like this in back of it, otherwise it runs all the risks heretofore encountered of exclusiveness or indefiniteness. But having said this one still feels the need to say more about form, about the form form takes in a novel, and about, as I suggested earlier, the provenance of form.

In *The Secular Scripture*, Frye makes a curious comment: "There are only so many ways of telling a story...." (*The Secular Scripture*, 9) In *Anatomy of Criticism*, he writes:

> The affinity between the mythical and the abstractly literary illuminates many aspects of fiction, especially the more popular fiction which is realistic enough to be plausible in its incidents and yet romantic enough to be a "good story," which means a clearly designed one. (139)

And again in *The Secular Scripture*:

> And yet, as we read *Pride and Prejudice* or *Emma* and ask the first question about it, which is: what is Jane Austen doing: what is it that drives her pen from one corner of the page to the other, the answer is of course that she is telling a story. The story is the soul of her writing, to use Aristotle's metaphor, the end for which all the words are put down. (39)

That is, over and above archetype and plausibility and heteroglossia, there remains the aspect of the novel, so far unexplored, that has to do with telling a story. Story has form; there are only "so many ways" of telling one. And perhaps it is not unreasonable to say that story form precedes any particular instance of story form, for example, the novel.

What Length Means for the Novel

The first thing to remark upon is that novels are long stories. The real significance of novel length dawned on me when I was doing research on the Iroquois for my novel *The Life and Times of Captain N.* Until then the only examples of great epics, national stories and creation myths I had encountered were things like *The Iliad* and *The Odyssey*, the *Bible*, and, say, *The Aeneid.* They were all relatively lengthy. But then I noticed that the only versions of the Iroquois creation stories I could find, the stories they recited regularly at their Longhouse religious services, were quite short, only a few pages long. I suddenly realized what a great divide there is between the world of oral myth and storytelling and the world of books.

The great epics I was familiar with had all been collected, compiled and written down long ago. They developed length as soon as they could be combined and threaded together, as soon as someone didn't have to remember them, as soon as they had been written down. In actual practice, epics and folktales had to be relatively short because they were limited by the ability of a human to commit them to memory. With the invention of writing and books (what Merlin Donald calls External Memory Devices), human memory began to lose its function as the primary storage area. Writing is actually much more dependable than memory.

Oral storytelling (and the storyteller) began to be replaced by much more solitary activities—writing and reading. A great religious crisis also occurred and is still occurring amongst all those peoples colonized by bookish invaders in the last thousand years. Sacred lore, myth and ritual that had been handed down orally and secretly from generation to generation began to lose its cachet. Writing sacred lore down meant that it would become public, lose its exclusivity, its sacred quality. (Along this line, it's possible to see the protestant schism with the Catholic Church as a development of book printing and mass literacy.) Many secrets were lost; what survives comes to us in the etiolate oral traditions of folklore and the fragments that managed to find their way into books.

No doubt the loss of dependence on human memory and the communal aspects of storytelling contributed to a culture-wide sense of loneliness (the subjective aspect of the rise of the individual—this is one of Marshall McLuhan's hobby-horses in *The Gutenberg Galaxy*). But with the invention of writing and books, more information could be stored and stories could grow longer. The novel, released from reliance on a limited human memory capacity, is a product of literacy, unthinkable without the alphabet.

The Invention of Plot

To me, this is a fascinating moment. When you've got a new technology and, suddenly, the possibility of making up longer narratives, well, at first you don't know quite what to do. You ask yourself: How do I write something that's long? The first option is simply to add more stories, one after the other (the anthology form), and maybe a frame. You invent a woman named Scheherazade and give her a problem that's solved by telling a new story every night, or you isolate a group of people in a country house where they hope to escape the plague and have them tell stories to pass the time. Or better yet (a clear advance) you adapt the quest motif and invent the road story, the picaresque, so that the new stories you keep adding to the book all happen to the same character. (You can see Rabelais beginning to realize how to combine love and the journey in the fourth book of his opus, when the company set off in a ship to seek the Oracle of the Holy Bottle—a woman—in order to solve Panurge's dilemma about whether to marry or not. The love and the journey are allegorical.)

One of the most exciting things about reading *Don Quixote* is that you get to see a writer grappling with the problem of length by inventing new forms and adapting old ones right before your eyes. First of all, it's a road story, a pseudo-quest as described above. Actually, the book seems to have started as a very short road story; Quixote is out and back on his first adventure in a few days, four and a half chapters. But then Cervantes must have thought, well, I can just have him go out on the road again, and, this time, I'll give him a partner, Sancho Panza, at which point something truly miraculous happens to the book (more on this when I get to the subject of subplots).

At the same time, Volume 1 of the novel, as Viktor Shklovsky points out in his essay on Cervantes in *Theory of Prose,* is very much a frame structure. Don Quixote has his adventures on the road, but much of the length comes from a great number of longish set-piece speeches, debates and inset stories, including the reading of a novel manuscript found in some left-luggage at an inn. Of course, Cervantes didn't invent this form; he was working in a tradition of transitional narratives that leads back to the dawn of written books.

To give a little context, here is Carolyn Lukens-Olson on Cervantes' very last book *Los trabajos de Persiles y Sigismunda*:

> ...*Persiles y Sigismunda* is short on battles and long on speeches. Well over one third of *Persiles y Sigismunda* is composed of speeches; the rest of the work is narration. Such a preponderance of speeches is not uncommon in the Byzantine romance and works written in that tradition. ("Heroics of Persuasion in *Los trabajos de Persiles y Sigismunda*" in *Cervantes: Bulletin of the Cervantes Society of America,* Fall, 2001, p51)

This makes sense if we regard the long story, call it romance or novel, as a form inventing itself out of a tradition of oral short forms, myths, legends, tales and, of course, public oratory and debate. At the outset, the old forms take centre stage and the frame, the narrative through-story, is scanted and cartoonish. In a footnote, Lukens-Olson writes:

> Hagg (294), for example, cites that nearly one half of Chariton's *Chaereas* is taken up in direct speech, monologues and dialogues, and Mack notes a similar format in Robert Greene's *Mamillia*, in which "The narrative is so often interspersed and augmented with speeches, soliloquies, letters and debates, and these texts are so much longer and more polished than the narrative that one reads the book more as an anthology of short texts than as a story." ("Heroics of Persuasion in *Los trabajos de Persiles y Sigismunda,*" 52n.; Hagg is Thomas Hagg who wrote *The Novel in Antiquity* and Mack is Peter Mack, editor of *Renaissance Rhetoric.*)

Chariton's *Chaereas and Callirhoë* is the earliest surviving Greek novel; he flourished, as they say, no later than the second century A.D. Robert Greene died in 1592. So we have here encapsulated (no doubt in a horribly over-simplified way) the genetic trajectory of the early novel leading up to Cervantes, the tradition out of which he developed.

Following the publication of Volume 1 of *Don Quixote*, certain critics took exception to the device of the inset stories, suggesting that the stories were tangential and interrupted the flow of the main story. As I have mentioned, Cervantes incorporates this criticism into the text of his novel:

> "One of the faults that are found with the history, added the batchelor, is, that the author has inserted in it, a novel intituled The Impertinent Curiosity? Not that the thing itself is bad, or poorly executed; but, because it is unreasonable, and has nothing to do with the story of his worship signor Don Quixote." (2,3)

Ten years later, when he published Volume 2, Cervantes had figured out how to cut back the number of inset stories and add length organically by developing aspects of the main story.

One of the things he does is invent a plot. This is a delicate point, not easy to express; for, of course, Cervantes had a plot of a sort in Volume 1, and stories had plots before *Don Quixote*. But in *Don Quixote*, Cervantes begins to teach us the rudiments of modern novel plotting. To recapitulate: the first solution to the problem of adding length is to add more stories and, possibly, a simple framing story. In the picaresque or road novel, the frame has developed into a story that runs the length of the book. We still get the inset stories but now they are motivated a bit better within the plot—the main character keeps meeting people along the way who tell him their stories. And the main character has an episodic series of adventures of his own. To some extent this is the structure we find in Volume 1 of *Don Quixote*.

The next development in novel composition occurs when the actual road is replaced as a unifying device by a consistent and singular desire. This is true plot and the structure on which most modern novels are based. So we move through 1) multiple stories happening to different people, to 2) multiple stories with a frame,

111

to 3) multiple stories with the road journey (the quest is a version of this) as a frame, some of the stories happening to the same character (the protagonist), to 4) multiple stories happening to the same character, all the stories being motivated and connected along a line of unitary desire. The road story doesn't disappear, of course, as the novel changes; even today the road remains a useful spatial metaphor for the thread of desire, the thread of plot, running through a book.

Here is what Cervantes in the voice of his narrator, who is giving us the thoughts of Cid Hamet Benengeli, has to say on the subject of the structural changes between Volume 1 and Volume 2. This comes from the opening of Chapter 44 in Volume 2, just as Sancho is about to separate from his master to attend to his new government in Barataria—what follows is a series of eight chapters alternating between Quixote and Sancho. In other words, this is precisely the spot at which Sancho, the subplot, sets out on his own as a parallel but structurally related storyline. One might say, in fact, that the modern novel is born in this passage.

> ...Cid Hamet Benengeli, who bewails his fate in having undertaken such a dry and confined history as that of Don Quixote; which obliged him to treat of nothing but the knight and his squire, without daring to launch out into other more grave and entertaining episodes, and digressions. He complained, that to be thus restricted in his hand, his pen, and his invention, to one subject only, so as to be obliged to speak through the mouths of a few persons, was insupportable toil, that produced no fruit to the advantage of the author; and that, in order to avoid this inconvenience, he had in the first part used the artifice of some novels, such as the Impertinent Curiosity, and the Captive, which were detached from the history although many particulars there recounted are really incidents which happened to Don Quixote; and, therefore, could not be suppressed. It was likewise his opinion, as he observes, that many readers being wholly ingrossed with the exploits of Don Quixote, would not bestow attention upon the novels, but pass them over either with negligence or disgust, without adverting to the spirit or artifice they contain; a truth

which would plainly appear, were they to be published by themselves, independent of the madness of Don Quixote, and the simplicities of Sancho. He would not therefore insert in the second part any novels, whether detached or attached; but only a few episodes that seem to spring from those very incidents which truth presents; and, even these, as brief and concise as they could possibly be related.... (2,44)

The use of the word "truth" just at the end is very curious. Cervantes must mean the truth of the book itself just as earlier he mentions incidents that "really" happened to Quixote. "Truth" in this sense refers to the structural confines that the author sets for himself; and these confines are what we have come to mean by novel form. They relate directly to rules of focus, economy and repetition as they relate to plot construction. As a matter of practice and experience teaching fiction writing, I have come to characterize plot as a sequence of events in which the same desire, in the heart of a leading character, meets the same resistance over and over again. When teaching story form, I tell my students that by story

> I mean a narrative that extends through a set of articula-
> tions, events or event sequences, in which the central con-
> flict is embodied once, and again, and again (three is the
> critical number here—looking back at the structure of
> folktales) such that in these successive revisitings we are
> drawn deeper into the soul or moral structure of the story.
> ("Notes on Story Structure" *The New Quarterly*, Number
> 87)

The key word here is the word "same," and I suspect the word "same" in this context is related to Cervantes' use of the word "truth" in the preceding quotation. Desire, resistance and conflict are standard components of a dramatic action; but successful plot construction requires the repetition of the same dramatic con-figuration through a series of event steps. The formal demand is alarmingly simple and rigorous, though it is always balanced aes-thetically by an equally powerful demand for variation. A literary work exists in a state of tension or dance between these paradoxical motions.

A story is written or a narrative surface is constructed with two concerns in mind: 1) the need to satisfy expectation, that is the need to fulfill the requirements of form, and I believe literature is a process of thinking with its own peculiar form, which the reader has come to know without consciously knowing it; and 2) the need to create interest, i.e. interest within the text, through variation of form, surprising turns or denials of expectation, dramatic action and emotional resonance. ("Notes on Story Structure")

The difference between an episodic narrative and a mature novel is that in the less rigorously constructed episodic form each event amounts to a separate story with separate desire and resistance structures whereas in a true novel plot the protagonist pursues the same desire through a series of encounters with the same resistance. This desire pattern creates the virtual road or thread that unites the events of the narrative into a single story.

A corollary of this is that it's possible to compose repetitions of the same events into the structure of a novel. For example, Quixote twice thinks his virtue is under attack by amorous maidens—Maritornes in Volume 1 and the bespectacled duenna in Volume 2. Similarly, in Volume 2, Quixote descends into a cave, and, many chapters later, so does Sancho. This is a variation of the structure that has the same event happening first in the main plot and later in the subplot. We can be sure Cervantes knew exactly what he was doing because he supplies a line that ties the two events together. "At least," says Sancho, "I shall not be so lucky as my master Don Quixote de la Mancha, who, when he descended into the cave of that same inchanted Montesinos...." (2,55)

The novel in general is thus a machine of desire. I don't mean simply sexual desire, though romantic attraction has been one of the prime subjects of the novel from the beginning. My sense of the structure is that novels are strung on a pure thread of desire, a single desire, insisting upon itself in the person of a character. Novels depart radically from real life itself by reason of this obsessive focus. Characters in novels resemble obsessive-compulsives more than ordinary people. It's a common mistake of the strict realist school of novel theory to assume that story and plot are devices of verisimilitude. In truth, novels stick to a single desire line in a way life never does.

On the other hand, the novel's clarity about the primacy of desire is one of its principle attractions to readers. We read novels, we identify with their protagonists, not because they remind us of something that once happened to us or because they deliver a vividly realistic picture of another historical epoch or how airports are run in a crisis but because desire is the one universal attribute (Schopenhauer said this, and of course neither he nor I mean simple genital desire). When I think of novels and stories in this way I am reminded of Freud's idea of the clash of the Pleasure Principle and the Reality Principle in our infantile psyches. We all start out in an undifferentiated universe wanting warmth, food (breast) and love (a kind, warm, buxom woman saying encouraging nonsense words; Cervantes' description of Aldonza Lorenzo as a "hale, buxom" young woman should now echo in your mind). Then we encounter the world that says we can't have these things, not all at once, not right now, not without work first. Why? Because we're naughty (hence morality). We begin to substitute other objects for love (symbols) or as prerequisites for love (we learn to earn). We learn to temporize, strategize, interpret, imagine, lie, calculate, steal, trick and kill. This is why, in a certain sense, all novels are bildungsromans and they are all about being perverse if we take "perverse" to mean finding the indirect or symbolic route to the object of our desires. And in this sense also, all culture can be seen as a crystallization of myriad acts of perversion.

In a sense, one of Cervantes' most brilliant perceptions is to realize that the heroes of chivalric romances acted in ways so bizarre that they seem, to us, quite demented. Don Quixote's madness is only normal romance behaviour perceived from the viewpoint of an ironic observer, someone who understands that the way people behave in books isn't normal. He falls in love with a woman he knows is imaginary and goes about the country getting into fights in her honour.

Cervantes has it both ways: he critiques the new form while revelling in its conventions. Quixote is both a hero and a nut, and he's a nut because he's acting like a hero in a book. And everything the curate and the narrator say against chivalric romances is correct. But the point is (Cervantes' point, I think) that it's dumb to think novels have anything to do with reality in the first place (see

Nabokov *supra*). The assumption that books have to be realistic is just as nutty as Don Quixote imitating a character in a book in real life. But I digress....

In Volume 1 of *Don Quixote*, the plot structure remains closely tied to the plot structure of chivalric romances of which it is a parody, and, for the most part, these are road stories, tales of adventure piled one on top of the other, motivated by abstract ideals, feudal concepts of honour, love and loyalty. At the opening, Quixote dons his armour and sets off in pursuit of adventures in the name of his imaginary lover Dulcinea. Though he thinks of her occasionally (she's his nominal motive), he rarely focuses on her. His only active attempt to reach her involves sending Sancho with a letter to her from the Sierra Morena (1,25). When the episodic plot begins to flag, Cervantes interrupts it with inset stories (albeit on the love theme). Quixote is reduced, in places, to the role of auditor; sometimes he just sleeps off-stage while a story is told. But in Volume 2, the first thing he does, upon setting out, is ride to Toboso to see Dulcinea. Inventing this gambit, Cervantes makes the love plot infinitely more concrete than in Volume 1. Of course, Dulcinea doesn't exist; Quixote thinks she's been transformed into a rude country girl on a donkey. He spends the rest of the novel vainly trying to disenchant her.

In terms of focus and the proportion of text related to the Quixote-Dulcinea plot line, the difference between Volume 1 and Volume 2 is striking. In Volume 1, Quixote only tries to contact Dulcinea once, and later he has a brief moment of quandary when he realizes he must finish his assignment for the Princess Micomicona before he can be worthy of visiting his love. Though he thinks of Dulcinea and talks about her now and then, these two events in particular constitute the only action on the Quixote-Dulcinea plot line. At one point, he even flirts with the idea of marrying Dorotea in the guise of the Princess Micomicona (1,30). In other words, the main plot line is only sketched in and the loose structure is filled in with episodic road adventures (entertaining as they are) and inset stories.

But in Volume 2, scene after scene turns on the problem of Dulcinea's enchantment. In the discourse of the novel, Quixote actually "sees" Dulcinea three times: first as a country girl on a donkey, then in his dream in the cave of Montesinos, and finally during the hoax enacted at the Duke's castle. That none of these encounters constitutes a real meeting does nothing to diminish their psychic importance or their role in the aesthetic structure of the book. Twice Quixote defends Dulcinea's honour in battles, first against the Knight of Mirrors and then against the Knight of the White Moon (both knights really Sampson Carrasco). He defeats the Knight of Mirrors, but, when overthrown by the Knight of the White Moon, he chooses death rather than deny her beauty (an offer Carrasco refuses).

In the course of that hallucinatory hoax, when Quixote meets the Duke's retainers impersonating Dulcinea and Merlin, he is given to believe that Sancho can release his lover from her enchantment by whipping himself 3300 times; so he spends the ensuing chapters nagging, threatening and cajoling the understandably reluctant Sancho to get the job done. In Barcelona, his visit to the oracular talking head is warped around his desire to find out if he will ever see her again. And, in the penultimate chapter, the awful realization (*malum signum*) that he will never see Dulcinea is the catalyst that sets in motion his final decline, return to sanity, and death.

> These words no sooner reached the knight's ears, than turning to his squire, "Friend Sancho, said he, didst thou mark what the boy said? Though shalt never see it in all the days of thy life." "And what signifies what the boy says?" answered the squire. "What! replied the knight, dost not thou perceive that the words, applied to my concerns, signify, that I shall never behold Dulcinea?" (2,73)

In addition to inventing the enchanted Dulcinea desire line as a unifying device in the organic structure of the novel, Cervantes reworked his plot resistance in Volume 2. In Volume 1, the curate and the barber, Quixote's friends, provide the countering resistance to the old knight's chivalric career, that is, the resistance that is strategic in terms of plot. Quixote meets all sorts of resistance along the way but these are tactical resistances inscribed in the pattern of road adventures. The curate and the barber try to save Quixote from himself by burning his books and bricking up his library, then they chase after him into the Sierra Morena and collude with Dorotea to humour him, and finally they trap him in the enchanted cage and drag him home in a wagon. (Quixote never realizes that his friends, the curate and the barber, are after him. In his mind, his enemies are the wicked enchanters who dog his steps. Even within the context of the novel, neither Dulcinea nor the enchanters are real.) The curate's relentlessness, I think, provides the centrifugal force that holds Volume 1 together. The curate brings Quixote home, brings him back to earth. But again the proportions seem strange to a modern eye. There is very little text related to plot event in contrast with the amount of text related to inset stories, speeches, dialogues (for example, the curate and the canon talking about romances while Quixote languishes in his cage) and road adventures. As I've outlined it here, it's basically a three-step resistance distributed over roughly 400 pages.

In Volume 2, perhaps realizing that he has exhausted the plot possibilities of the curate and the barber alone, Cervantes adds the student, Sampson Carrasco, to the character grouping. In one sense, Carrasco is a new character, but in another sense he is just a variation on the curate-barber theme, that is, he's an interested party who humours Quixote in order to cure him of his insane fancies. The curate and the barber recede in significance and proportion of text. At the beginning of Volume 2, Carrasco brings news of the publication of Volume 1 of *Don Quixote*, and, in collusion with the curate, concocts the cockamamie scheme of encouraging the old knight to break out again as a knight errant so as to contrive his ultimate defeat. Then, disguised as the Knight of Mirrors and the Knight of the White Moon, he tracks Quixote through the countryside until defeating him on the beach at Barcelona. Again, the resistance works in three steps (in about 400 pages) and takes up, if anything, less text than in Volume 1. Where in Volume 1 Cervantes developed the curate in scenes with the barber and Quixote's niece, with the canon, with Dorotea, and so on, in Volume 2, he barely touches on Carrasco's life apart from his encounters with Quixote. Nevertheless, as Cervantes clearly knew, this three-step resistance is enough to carry the novel through to its conclusion.

The Invention of Subplot

The subplot is a crucial structure peculiar to the novel (as opposed to short stories). The longer a piece of narrative prose the more necessary a subplot or subplot-like device becomes. The following is an excerpt from a lecture I give when I'm teaching novel-writing to graduate students:

A subplot or subplot-like device is a distinguishing characteristic of the novel as opposed to the short story; you need at least one for a novel (of course, there are exceptions, but they are usually very short novels); in short stories you can do without them. In its simplest and most direct form the subplot is another plot, involving another set of characters, weaving through the novel (obviously, characters can and do act on both plot and subplot lines). Sometimes a subplot expands to about the same amount of text as the main plot and becomes a parallel plot.

As I say, you have to know how the main plot works in order to construct the subplot because the subplot has to bear a particular relationship to the main plot: it has to be congruent or antithetical. In *Anna Karenina*, the plot and parallel plot are opposites (and there is a third plot—the Oblonsky plot—which is congruent with the main plot). I know I make this sound a bit geometrical. Aldous Huxley in *Point Counter Point* has his novel-writing character describe it slightly differently: "A novelist modulates by reduplicating situations and characters. He shows several people falling in love, or dying, or praying in different ways—dissimilars solving the same problem. Or, *vice versa*, similar people confronted with dissimilar problems."

If the subplot bears the proper relation to the main plot, then you get the resonating or echoing effect that you want. To my mind, this subplot resonance is the key to what we call the "aliveness" of a novel—contrary to popular opinion which seems to hold that aliveness comes from verisimilitude, that quality of seeming to be real. Subplot resonance is also one of the ways of giving a novel the sense of being about a teeming world, about a lot of people, when it will most often be about a small group of people. In a little essay on *King Lear*, W. B. Yeats called the effect of subplotting "the emotion of multitudes."

> The Shakespearian drama gets the emotion of multitude out of the subplot which copies the main plot, much as a shadow upon the wall copies one's body in the firelight.... Lear's shadow is in Gloucester, who also has ungrateful children, and the mind goes on imagining shadows, shadow beyond shadow, till it has pictured the world. In Hamlet, one hardly notices, so subtly is the web woven, that the murder of Hamlet's father and the sorrow of Hamlet are shadowed in the lives of Fortinbras and Ophelia and Laertes, whose fathers, too, have been killed.

Generally, subplots involve a second or third set of characters who are closely related to the main set of characters. Tolstoy, in his letters, said he always used other family members as subplot characters. In *Anna Karenina*, the main plot is between Anna and Vronsky, the parallel plot is between Levin and Kitty, the smaller subplot is between Oblonsky (Anna's brother) and his wife (Kitty's sister). Anne Tyler uses family members in a novel like *The Accidental Tourist* (main plot—Macon and the dog trainer; subplot—Macon's sister and his editor; lesser subplot—Macon's brothers). But there is also the upstairs-downstairs novel where the plot and subplot are distributed among social classes (Shakespeare and Cervantes both construct subplots along this line, for example). And a group of friends or schoolmates or army buddies can provide the same opportunities (e.g. Mary McCarthy's *The Group*). The advantage of the near relations between characters on plot and subplot lines is that they can interact with and observe one another naturally. This mutual awareness creates opportunities for thematic commentary that cuts both ways. ("Notes on Novel Structure" *The New Quarterly*, Number 87)

I've said that something miraculous happens to the novel when Cervantes invents Sancho Panza and sends him on the road with his mournful master. The first four and a half chapters of Volume 1 are lonely and a bit quiet in comparison with everything that follows, all those pages filled with the endless comic chatter between the old knight and his squire. But the thing to realize first and foremost is that the subplot is a device of the long story. It's one of the ways of adding more stories to the main story while keeping the whole work organically coherent.

On a very simple level, in both Volume 1 and Volume 2, there are places where Quixote and Sancho split up and Sancho has his own adventures. In Volume 1, this happens when Quixote sends Sancho to deliver a letter to Dulcinea; Sancho meets the curate and barber at the oft-mentioned inn and joins with their plan to trick Quixote into returning home. But Cervantes reinvents the structure in Volume 2 where Sancho plays a much greater role in the main plot but also develops a real plot of his own; that is, he becomes governor of the island of Barataria (achieves his desire) and, after some days, decides that being a governor is not what he really wants and resigns. In doing so, he achieves a wisdom and dignity that has hitherto been lacking in his character. In a sense, he wrestles himself out of the bad dream of the novel plot, something Quixote himself is never quite able to do. In the last chapter, Quixote simply reverts to sanity as suddenly as, at the beginning of the book, he went mad.

I have already discussed the plot and subplot structure of the novel in a earlier segment of this essay, but it's worth looking just a bit more carefully at the technique and craft involved. Through the plot and subplot structure Quixote and Sancho are yoked together, almost always in some variant of the relation of ironic contrast. Quixote is a gentleman, Sancho is a peasant; Quixote is a virgin, Sancho is married with children; Quixote is a reader, Sancho is illiterate (on the other hand, Quixote tries to send letters to his mistress and never succeeds, and Sancho manages to exchange lively letters with his wife); Quixote's structural desire is for the imaginary Dulcinea, Sancho's is to govern an island as his portion of the spoils of knight-errantry; Quixote is an insomniac, Sancho likes to sleep; Quixote eats sparingly, whereas Sancho loves to eat; Quixote, though a virgin, thinks of himself as passionate and is often comically fearful for his virtue in the presence of women, whereas Sancho never seems to notice them.

Not only are they linked in terms of their partnership in actions and events along the plot line, but Cervantes is constantly linking and measuring them syntactically, as in this moment when, just before Sancho departs to take up his position as governor of Barataria, Quixote says:

> "I return infinite thanks to heaven, friend Sancho, for having ordained, that, before I myself have met with the least success, good fortune hath gone forward to bid thee welcome. I, who had ballanced the remuneration of thy service in my own prosperity, find myself in the very rudiments of promotion; while thou, before thy time, and contrary to all laws of reasonable progression, findest thy desire accomplished...." (2,42)

It's interesting to note that in this passage Quixote is himself aware of the parallel and contrast pattern of the two plots, is meditating on their relationship in his own mind. Whereas sometimes the links are made by the narrator. For example, just after the episode of the talking head, Cervantes reminds us again of the parallel desires and calibrates their relative progress.

> ...and the result of all his reflections, was the promise of Dulcinea's being disinchanted, on which he reposed himself with the most implicit confidence. This was the goal of all his thoughts, and he rejoiced, in full assurance of seeing it suddenly accomplished; and, as for Sancho, although he abhorred the office of governor, as we have already observed, he could not help wishing for another opportunity of issuing out orders and seeing them obeyed.... (2,63)

Earlier, just after Quixote and Sancho are rescued from the mill-race, we find an example of the linkage beginning in the narrative and shifting subtly into Sancho's mind (note again how the text is always measuring distance from the goal, and, in this passage, how Sancho's subplot point of view works to reflect on the main plot):

At length, they mounted, in the most profound silence, and departed from the banks of that famous river, Don Quixote buried as it were amidst the meditations of his love, and Sancho immersed in those of his preferment, which, at that time, seemed to be a weary distance; for, maugre all his simplicity and folly, he could easily perceive that all, or the greatest part, of his master's actions, proceeded from frenzy and distraction: he therefore resolved to take an opportunity of retreating abruptly to his own house.... (2,30)

And here is a fascinating example of the syntactical linkage between Sancho and Quixote from a fourth structural vantage point, that is, the point of view of the resistance or counter-plot. The quotation is from Teresa's letter to Sancho:

Sampson vows he will go in quest of thee, and drive this government out of thy head, as well as the madness out of Don Quixote's skull.... (2,52)

This is the nuts and bolts connective tissue of plot and subplot writing, the insertion of textual connectors and tie-ins, the insistence upon parallel desires.

On a more trivial level, Cervantes continues the pattern whenever the opportunity arises, as in:

"Eat, friend Sancho, said Don Quixote, and support life, which is of more importance to thee than to me, and leave me to die by the strength of imagination and the severity of my misfortunes. I, Sancho, was born to live dying, and thou to die eating...." (2,59)

...one of whom [Sancho] the new day found sleeping at full snore, and the other [Quixote] watching over his disastrous thoughts, and very impatient to quit his couch; for, whether vanquished or victor, Don Quixote never took pleasure in lolling in the hay. (2,70)

And, of course, there is the constant bickering over Sancho's proverbs and malapropisms (which theme achieves a sort of symmetry or balance when Quixote himself begins to speak in proverbs late in the novel.)

Sancho and Quixote are the same yet different, Cervantes keeps reminding us, with similar or parallel structural roles and quite different physical and social attributes, the same melody but in a different key, as Madariaga says. Or, they might be thought of as doubles, the one born out of the other by a sort of literary parthenogenesis, but with their personal characteristics shaded or graded differently. As Sancho says, as he is about to leave Quixote and fulfill his desire of becoming governor of an island, "If your worship will consider, your worship will find, that you yourself put this scheme of government into my head...." (2,43)

In the chapters following, Cervantes alternates between the Sancho/Barataria plot and the Quixote plot (his adventures with Altisidora, the cats and Donna Rodriguez). Chapters 45, 47, 49, 51 and 53 are all about Sancho and his government. Chapter 54 recounts what happened to Sancho on his way back to Don Quixote and includes the inset story of Ricote, the expelled Morisco. In Chapter 55, Sancho falls into a cave (parallelled with Quixote dropping into the cave of Montesinos). Part-way through the chapter, Cervantes shifts from Sancho's story to Quixote's story: "Here Cid Hamet Benengeli, leaving the squire, returns to Don Quixote...." A couple of paragraphs later the two plots reconverge when Quixote, out for a morning ride, hears Sancho's faint calls from inside the cave. Between times, the two plots remain subtly conscious of one another, that is, they think of one another (and Quixote writes to Sancho, Sancho includes messages to Quixote in his letters to the Duke, and Quixote reads the letters Sancho and Teresa send to one another).

Though the plots now run on together, there is still a clear sense in which Sancho and Quixote experience their adventures differently; the plot and subplot, though contiguous, remain distinct. The last act of both comes as the two characters return to the village from which they set out. Once again the two plots are syntactically linked, this time in a paragraph (2,73). The paragraph begins and ends with Quixote, his housekeeper, his niece, the curate and Carrasco grouped in silence. But most of the paragraph is taken up with the noisy, tempestuous, affectionate and over-poweringly physical welcome accorded Sancho by his family. The contrast is poignant and telling.

In a word, they entered the town, surrounded with boys, and accompanied by the curate and the batchelor, who attended them to the knight's house, at the gate of which they found the niece and the housekeeper already apprized of his arrival. The same intimation, neither more nor less, had been given to Sancho's spouse Teresa Panza, who came running to see her husband, half naked, with her hair hanging about her ears, and her daughter Sanchica in her hand: but, seeing he was not so gayly equipped, as she thought a governor should be, "Heyday! husband, cried she, you come home afoot, and seem to be quite foundered, and look more like a governor of hogs than a ruler of men." "Hold your tongue, Teresa, replied the squire; you will often find hooks where there is no bacon: let us e'en trudge home, where I will tell thee wonders: I have money in my purse (and that's the one thing needful) earned by my own industry, without prejudice to any person whatsoever." "Do you bring home the money, good husband, said Teresa: and let it be earned here or there, or got in what shape you please, I give myself no trouble about the matter; I am sure, in getting it, you have introduced no new fashion into the world." Sanchica embraced her father, and asked if he had brought anything for her, who had expected him as impatiently as if he had been May-dew: then taking hold of his girdle with one hand, and leading Dapple with the other, while her mother held him by the fist, they repaired to their own house, leaving Don Quixote to the care of his niece and housekeeper, and in company with the curate and batchelor.

Quixote's love for Dulcinea is ultimately a sterile, lonely affair, blocked by her non-existence, by his vow of chastity and by its being only an imitation love to begin with; the gap is inscribed in the desire itself. The contrast the novel offers to Quixote's predicament is the socially sanctioned institution of marriage; this is very clear in the twinned relationship of plot and subplot, Quixote and Sancho. In contrast to Quixote's chivalric adventuring, Sancho's marriage is, well, a marriage. He confers with his wife Teresa, asks her advice, bickers with her, sends her gifts, worries about her, compromises for her, is proud of her, is faithful to her, depends on her, and, in the end, has a pretty realistic picture of her which shocks Don Quixote who prefers his relationships on the ideal level.

"What, is Teresa such a bad wife?" said the knight. "Not very bad, answered the squire, but, then she is not very good; at least, not so good as I could wish." "You are in the wrong, Sancho, said Don Quixote, to disparage your wife, who in effect is the mother of your children." "As to that matter, replied Sancho, we are not at all in one another's debt; for, she can disparage me fast enough, especially when she takes it in her head to be jealous, and then Satan himself could not endure her." (2,22)

Where Don Quixote claims to be dying for love ("I am dying with desire" (2,60)), that Dulcinea is the "sole mistress of my thoughts" (2,58), Sancho says,

"...never in my born days did I know a lacemaker die from love: the thoughts of girls employed at that work, run more upon the finishing of their tasks than upon the idle fancies of love; and, for myself, I can safely say, that while I am digging in the field, I never so much as dream of my duck; I mean, my wife Teresa Panza, whom I love as the apple of mine eye." (2,70)

And though Quixote is eloquent and literate, he never manages to exchange a word with the woman he loves (either Dulcinea or Aldonza Lorenzo); while illiterate Sancho, who has barely learned to recognize the numbers inscribed on donkey packs, carries on a lively correspondence with the Duke and Duchess, Quixote, and, especially, his equally illiterate wife Teresa. And where Quixote's final homecoming is steeped in silence, Sancho's, as I have mentioned, is noisy, bumptious and physically affectionate.

The contrast, as I say, is poignant and pointed, especially at the end, though I don't think it means we should read Cervantes as a poster child for the institution of marriage and family values. (*Anna Karenina*, in which Tolstoy deploys a similar plot-subplot contrast—i.e. Levin's marriage against Anna's adultery—does in comparison suffer from a certain moralizing quality.) No doubt the ideal of domestic, tribal bliss is as much a fantasy as the chivalrous ideal;

nor is Sancho, as we have seen, impervious to the seductions of desire. If Quixote views the world through a prism skewed by the chivalric romances he reads, Sancho sees it through a prism clouded with all those folk sayings and truisms he spouts. The marriage contrast is meant to throw Quixote's plot into relief, to give it a ground, to use McLuhan's metaphor. But it also serves as an ironic corrective to the old knight's romantic and rhetorical flights of fancy.

Marriage and ideal love are different styles of approach to the issue of the other. Marriage, aside from all the sacramental mumbo-jumbo, is the image of a pragmatic unity of conjoined individuals; it is, in a sense, the antithesis of desire. It is not about reaching; it's about grappling with the other. Marriage may not even be about love, if by love we mean that insatiable thirst that no particular other person, no real other, can quench. Working at love seems like an oxymoron, but marriage counselling makes sense. Marriage is about compromise, negotiation and translation. If love is to be explained in terms of ideals, marriage is about property, nurturing children, a division of labour and a commitment to social order. When Quixote and Sancho speak of love, they are talking different languages.

This is technically how plot and subplot work. The author sets up parallel structures and runs them side by side through the novel, sometimes bringing them together, sometimes letting them step apart, weaving connective material between them, constantly reminding the reader of the thematic relationship, and allowing the characters on one plot to think of characters on the other plot, commenting, echoing, vibrating. You can see Rabelais fumbling to invent the same device, but Panurge, instead of developing into a subplot character, actually begins to take over as the character of primary concern; Rabelais' structure is sequential rather than simultaneous, inorganic and broken-backed, and not quite successful as a novel.

By the same token, I wouldn't say Cervantes invented the subplot all on his own. The subplot is an outgrowth of the inset or added story and other, more archaic, oral devices of reflection and repetition. For example, Marshall McLuhan was fond of talking about a Greek rhetorical device called the epyllion (the little epic, a version of *ekphrasis*) which he thought of as akin to the subplot.

(Marchand, *Marshall McLuhan*, 265) And in drama, the Greek chorus had a somewhat analogous role, intermittent and reflective. I suspect the device of the subplot in the novel grew out of more antique structures such as these and migrated to the novel from the theatre (at the same time Cervantes was inventing Quixote, Shakespeare was constructing plays using the plot and subplot structure at the peak of sophistication).

Character Grouping and Gradation

Character grouping and gradation are elements of novel structure often related to plot and subplot concerns. I have already mentioned it here and there in the preceding sections. Nabokov, ever reluctant to give into the charms of *Don Quixote* without a fight, is particularly scathing on this:

> We see here [the melée scene at the remarkable inn of coincident fates (1,45)]...a forlorn attempt on the author's part to group his characters according to their natures and emotions—to bring them in a group, but also keep them as individuals before the reader's eyes, so as to remind him all the time of their special features and have them act all together, without leaving anybody out. All this is quite clumsy and inartistic.... (*Lectures on Don Quixote*, 39)

Actually, I am not quite sure what Nabokov is objecting to. The scene in question is a bit of a farce, with characters from several separate inset stories converging violently on one another. There is little room here for the real novelistic art of character grouping at which Cervantes in fact excels. And when Nabokov lists character groups, he collects them according to the stories in which they participate rather than in terms of shared character traits.

By character grouping I mean the composition of characters based on shared traits; these traits are varied, diminished or intensified from one character to another, that is, they are graded. Another way of saying this is to remember how Madariaga thought of

Sancho as the same as Quixote only transposed into a different key. Character gradation is a subject E. K. Brown touches on in his brilliant little book *Rhythm in the Novel*. Here he is discussing the two daughters, Anastasie and Delphine in Balzac's *Le Père Goriot*. Note how this echoes my earlier discussion of Sancho's linkage to Quixote.

> ...Anastasie is dark and Delphine fair; Anastasie married for rank and has almost the manners of the Faubourg Saint-Germain (though she does not live in it), Delphine married for money and has the manners of a banker's wife from the Chausée d'Antin. If you listen to the scandal about them, it would not tell the same story: Anastasie was thought to give money to her lover, Delphine to take it from hers. None of these variations touches the core of these characters....
>
> The daughters are alike at the core, the very same indeed, because they are products of the same circumstance, the deplorable upbringing their idolatrous father gave them.... Anastasie and Delphine make the same kinds of demand on their father; and put the same kind of humiliation on him. Only so can Balzac render his theme with the fullest emphasis, and prevent the reader's escaping from the impact he intends. If Père Goriot had had only one ravenously selfish daughter, the reader might have said: "No, it was not her upbringing that ruined her, there was something ineradicably corrupt inside her for which her father was not answerable. He was guiltless." But if there are two ravenously selfish daughters, and no others, and if they are selfish in exactly the same way, the guilt is fixed elsewhere. (*Rhythm in the Novel*, 21-22)

Another great example of character grouping and gradation, on a similar theme, can be found in Jane Austen's novel *Mansfield Park* in which the Bertram children, two brothers and two sisters, all suffer from being spoiled and indulged by their wealthy, but distant father. The effects of their being spoiled work out differently in each child, from Edmund who is kindly yet blind to real affection (though he wakes up in time to marry Fanny Price in the end), to Tom who piles up debt through dissipation, to Julia who elopes with a second-rate man, to Maria who marries for money and ruins her life completely by running off with a lover.

To make the theme absolutely clear, Austen introduces a second family, and a second set of children, similarly blighted by a bad upbringing. Henry and Mary Crawford, having lost their mother, are brought up in the home of an uncle, who, though wealthy, is "a man of vicious conduct" who lives openly with his mistress. Mary Crawford is lovely, tempts Edmund yet inevitably proves herself morally unsound; but Henry is an outrageous flirt, maliciously careless of the lives he toys with. After almost convincing Fanny to fall in love with him, Henry runs off with the married Maria Bertram. Thus the novel is constructed around a group of six young people, all alike at their core, but expressing their moral weaknesses in varying degrees and to different effects.

This is exactly the kind of pattern we have found in *Don Quixote*. Sancho and Quixote are both gentle hearts easily carried away by their enthusiasm for preposterous ideals. They are both earnest and naive, both easy marks for the elaborate hoaxes perpetrated on them. Their goals are parallel, though different, and the upshot of each of their plots is also varied: Sancho discovers his true self and returns to the bosom of his family while Quixote recovers his sanity and dies. But the technique of grouping and gradation extends itself throughout the novel. Other groups include the resistance or counter-plot group (the curate, the barber and Sampson Carrasco); the real and spurious Sancho and Quixote group; the hoaxing group (the Duke and Duchess, Dorotea, the curate and barber, etc.); the victims of Don Quixote's rash attacks group; and even the Panza family group—

> The curate hearing her remark, "I cannot believe, said he, but that all the family of the Panzas are born with a bag of proverbs in their bowels; for, I have never seen one of them, who does not scatter about old saws, at all times, and in all conversations." (2,50)

The effect of character grouping and gradation is, like many of the other structures we've been looking at, to create a thematic and structural cohesiveness, a critical intensity of focus that prevents the long story (with all those extra characters) from sprawling and dissipating its energy. It reinforces theme and strangely enough seems to give the characters a special clarity. Here is how Brown describes the effect in Henry James' novels:

> Each of these persons irradiates the others, and each becomes clearer by irradiation. By this irradiation the Jamesian scene assumes the soft contours of life.... (*Rhythm in the Novel*, 27)

The Nudge

This leads me to a further point of conjecture. I have always been curious about the ten-year gap between the two parts of the book. Cervantes promised a sequel as soon as he finished Volume 1 but somehow couldn't get to it. The standard explanation is that he cared more about his plays and exemplary novels and the love-adventure story he thought was his masterpiece, *Persiles y Sigismunda*. Let the words of John Ormsby, in the introduction to his translation of *Quixote*, represent the standard explanation:

> He shows plainly enough, too, that *Don Quixote* and the demolition of the chivalry romances was not the work that lay next his heart. He was, indeed, as he says himself in his preface, more a stepfather than a father to *Don Quixote*. Never was great work so neglected by its author. That it was written carelessly, hastily, and by fits and starts, was not always his fault, but it seems clear he never read what he sent to the press.... He appears to have regarded the book as little more than a mere *libro de entretenimiento*, an amusing book, a thing, as he says in the *Viaje*, "to divert the melancholy moody heart at any time or season." No doubt he had an affection for his hero, and was very proud of Sancho Panza. It would have been strange indeed if he had not been proud of the most humorous creation in all fiction. He was proud, too, of the popularity and success of the book, and beyond measure delightful is the naïveté with which he shows his pride in a dozen passages in the

Second Part. But it was not the success he coveted. In all probability he would have given all the success of *Don Quixote*, nay, would have seen every copy of *Don Quixote* burned in the Plaza Mayor, for one such success as Lope de Vega was enjoying on an average once a week.

And so he went on, dawdling over *Don Quixote*, adding a chapter now and again, and putting it aside to turn to *Persiles and Sigismunda*—which, as we know, was to be the most entertaining book in the language, and the rival of *Theagenes and Chariclea*—or finishing off one of his darling comedies; and if Robles [the printer/publisher] asked when *Don Quixote* would be ready, the answer no doubt was: En brève—shortly, there was time enough for that.

But, as Ormsby says, Nemesis, in the form of the anonymous author of the spurious sequel, *Second Volume of the Ingenious Gentleman Don Quixote of La Mancha: by the Licentiate Alonso Fernandez de Avellaneda of Tordesillas*, was working in the wings. According to Ormsby, the vicious, mocking tone of the author's preface, more than the simple threat of competition, goaded Cervantes into finishing his own novel. And the threat of other anonymous authors reworking his material prompted Cervantes to kill off his hero at the end of Volume 2 rather than leave open the possibility of a continuation.

But whatever Avellaneda and his book may be, we must not forget the debt we owe them. But for them, there can be no doubt, *Don Quixote* would have come to us a mere torso instead of a complete work. Even if Cervantes had finished the volume he had in hand, most assuredly he would have left off with a promise of a Third Part, giving the further adventures of Don Quixote and humours of Sancho Panza as shepherds. It is plain that he had at one time an intention of dealing with the pastoral romances as he had dealt with the books of chivalry, and but for Avellaneda he would have tried to carry it out. But it is more likely that, with his plans, and projects, and hopefulness, the volume would have remained unfinished till his death, and that we should have never made the acquaintance of the Duke and Duchess, or gone with Sancho to Barataria.

From the moment the book came into his hands he seems to have been haunted by the fear that there might be more Avellanedas in the field, and putting everything else aside, he set himself to finish off his task and protect Don Quixote in the only way he could, by killing him. The conclusion is no doubt a hasty and in some places clumsy piece of work and the frequent repetition of the scolding administered to Avellaneda becomes in the end rather wearisome; but it is, at any rate, a conclusion and for that we must thank Avellaneda.

Ormsby's conjecture is quite possibly correct insofar as Cervantes' motives are concerned (it's ironic that in the first chapter of Volume 1, Cervantes describes Quixote himself contemplating writing a sequel to someone else's novel), but I wonder if motive constitutes the whole story. There is often a gap between what writers want to do and what they can do in terms of technical invention. And writers tend to keep on with projects, especially money-making projects, unless they just can't figure out where to go with them. If we think of a novel as a problem of structure and length and then examine Cervantes' composition more carefully, another explanation might manifest itself.

Volume 1 begins with that 4½-chapter, abortive first adventure. No Sancho, subplot, no continuous resistance, just a brief run of disastrous scrapes for the old knight. Cervantes then realized he could extend the original story by simply having Quixote break out again, that is, by simply re-telling the same story. But he needed to create some variation and imagine a way of extending the extension, as it were, technically. He invented Sancho (subplot), hit upon a method of working the curate and the barber into the novel as a continuous resistance (while Quixote wanders about, they are relentlessly on his trail—a baroque version of *Butch Cassidy and the Sundance Kid*), and bulked up the huff-and-puff against chivalric romances. He then added the inset stories and the various road-skirmishes. But, by the end of Volume 1, he had exhausted these possibilities; his structure needed to be refreshed. (And there were those critics who took him to task for leaning so heavily on the inset-story technique.)

I am speculating, fabricating, if you want to say that (though no more than Ormsby does), since there really isn't any evidence one way or the other for what was on Cervantes' mind. I offer this fable as a counter to the standard fiction because the standard fiction makes Cervantes out to be naive and a little dumb about his own work. I suspect Cervantes was working on the continuation of Volume 1 all the time he was writing other things, working in that secondary sense of the word peculiar to artists whose work includes dry spells, long bouts with boredom, and tangential activities; he just couldn't crack the code. And then, like a gift from God, the spurious sequel came along and handed him the key.

A book often needs a nudge, a spur under the saddle, something to be cranky about (this is a formal demand, not a moral one). The nudge in Volume 1 is the animus against chivalric romances, a general animus situated in the minds of the authorial first-person narrator and several characters including the curate and the barber. And to a certain extent this motive carries over into Volume 2, especially in the last few lines of the novel where it is emphatically reasserted by Cid Hamet Benengeli. But coming to this same material a second time, Cervantes must have felt how thin and flat it would feel to hang another 400 pages on the same coatrack. The spurious sequel gave him a substitute, and a substitute that actually functioned in a more focused and organic way because it was now felt as a threat in Don Quixote's own mind. But Cervantes had to wait till his anonymous competitor's real novel suggested itself as a possible literary device.

Within the structural possibilities of novel form, it's fascinating then to see what Cervantes does with his new nudge. In Volume 1, the animus against chivalric romances doesn't directly eventuate in plot elements after the burning of Alonso Quixano's library. There are, yes, several scenes of speechifying and dialogue (e.g. between the curate and the canon) on the subject of bad literature, but these are presentations of argument rather than plot. In Volume 2, the spurious sequel to Volume 1 transforms itself into a secondary plot, another subplot: another knight named Don Quixote with another squire named Sancho Panza are wandering about Spain. The spurious Don Quixote actually reaches Saragossa before the real Don Quixote precipitating his decision to forego the tournament there and ride for Barcelona instead. Later, Don Quixote makes the acquaintance of a man who knows the impostor (one isn't quite sure what to call him). And the existence of this second Don Quixote clearly provokes anxiety and melancholy in the old knight, adding to the cares, slights, humiliations and debacles that dog his steps through the final pages of the book and conduce to his final breakdown.

Note once more Cervantes' use of character grouping and gradation. To use Madariaga's metaphor yet again: Quixote and Sancho are alike but in different keys just as the impostor knight and squire are like the real knight and squire but sounded in a different key. The spurious Don Quixote turns out to be the opposite of the real Don Quixote in every respect except for his name and the name of his fat companion, indeed he becomes the "bad Don Quixote." (2,72) Don Alvaro Tarfe has "saved his back from being very roughly handled by the hangman, for his excessive impudence and knavery." And the spurious Sancho turns out, contrary to reports, to be rather humourless.

> "...I am of the same opinion, replied Don Alvaro; for, truly, my good friend, you have uttered more pleasantry in these few sentences you have spoke, than ever I knew come from the mouth of the other Sancho Panza, tho' he was an eternal babbler: he was much more of a glutton than an orator, and rather idiotical than humourous. (2,72)

Note how clear it is that such structures (subplots, groups of characters, and gradation) develop through a simple doubling or splitting process. Characters in novels replicate by cell division. They split off a semblance of themselves with the various characteristics shaded differently, either exaggerated or diminished. Thus the curate and the barber are a pair, though one is clearly more educated and more officially significant. The two of them spawn a younger, more energetic version of themselves in the person of Sampson Carrasco. Don Quixote spawns Sancho, an illiterate, tubbier, plain-speaking, lower-class version of himself, who nonetheless buys into the dream of knight-errantry, albeit in terms of its material rather than its spiritual prospects. And Don Quixote and Sancho spawn a knight and squire with identical names who are knavish, stupid and gluttonous. Herein we see a certain sort of compositional or aesthetic logic in play and it's this logic which, I think, is another way of defining what Cervantes means by "truth" in the passage I mentioned earlier in my discussion of plot structure:

> He would not therefore insert in the second part any novels, whether detached or attached; but only a few episodes that seem to spring from those very incidents which truth presents.... (2,44)

Novel Form and Memory

The invention of the book severed the archaic direct connection between human memory and stories. But as stories grew longer some backward accommodation had to be made with the limits of ordinary human memory. Techniques (forms) needed to be invented that would help the reader, in some fashion, keep the whole book in mind. Oral stories tend to be confined not only to what can be memorized (brief, repetitive, given to stock phrasing and epithets, employing flat or generalized character types) but also to what can be told in a single sitting. Books are read over several sittings, sometimes put down and picked up over weeks or months. But beyond that most novels are just too long to hold in memory, even in the generalized and somewhat vague short-term memory that seems to make up an essential part of the act of reading. So what we discover in terms of forms that are peculiar to the modern novel (though obviously they have spread also to the modern short story, memoir, etc.) is a range of techniques that give the long story a memory, techniques of repetition, rehearsal and review. This range of techniques extends from simple repetition to larger structural devices. Simple repetition might involve an image as in Volume 2, Chapter 73, when Don Quixote and Sancho return to their village at the novel's close, and Cervantes uses an image tie-back to remind us of an earlier event (2,69).

> Now the reader must know, that Sancho Panza had, over the bundle of armour carried by Dapple, thrown, by way of a sumptercloth, the buckram robe painted with flames of

fire, which he had worn in the Duke's castle, on the night of Altisidora's resurrection....

Or it might involve a transitional tie-back in the narrative itself, that is, in the voice of the narrator.

> We left the great governor [Sancho as governor of Barataria] out of humour, and enraged at the same painting country-wag, who had received his cue from the duke's steward and gentleman sewer, sent hither on purpose to make merry at his expence.... (2,49)

And again:

> Cid Hamet, the most punctual investigator of the most minute atoms belonging to this genuine history, says that when Donna Rodriguez quitted her apartment to visit Don Quixote.... (2,50)

Each of these techniques falls under the general heading of what I call substitute memories. In *Lectures on Don Quixote*, Nabokov talks about two larger structural devices which fit under the same rubric.

> An important note of structure: Cervantes for the sake of keeping the novel together (it threatens to sprawl at this point [1,31]), has the characters either recall past events or has characters from former chapters appear again. Thus on his errand to Dulcinea, Sancho passes through the village where he has been blanket-tossed. Thus the galley-slaves are mentioned by the priest; thus the robber who stole Sancho's ass appears again in a gypsy's garb; thus the lad whom Don Quixote had attempted to save from the brutal farmer clasps the good knight's knees again. The continuation of these episodes along the main current of the story (which after all began with the bubbles of parody and then flowed on as an account of a pathetic and noble creature's mad fancies)—the continuations and development of these episodes along the main current do give the story the kind of sweeping unity that in our minds is associated with the form of the novel. (*Lectures on Don Quixote*, 141-142)

Nabokov here gives several examples of the returning character technique from Volume 1. There are plenty of examples of recalling past events as well. I'll just touch on a few from Volume 2. In Chapter 51, Sancho sits in judgment in his "island" kingdom of Barataria. He does so well his courtiers exclaim their admiration, and he tells them:

> "...Nor, indeed, have I spoken my own sentiment on the occasion; but, I have recollected one, among the many precepts I received from my master Don Quixote, the very night I set out for the government of this island: he said, that when justice was doubtful, I should choose, and lean towards mercy...." (2,51)

The conversation referred to here took place in Chapter 43. This device, what I call a tie-back, seems so natural and appropriate in its context that I think readers and critics have a difficult time noticing what a crucial role it plays in the construction of a novel text.

At the opening of the next chapter, we find another type of tying-together device. This one is fascinating because it ties back to the previous chapter but also ties forward by announcing Quixote's plan for the immediate future. The chapter begins:

> Cid Hamet recounts, that Don Quixote now being cured of his scratches, began to think the life he led in the castle was altogether contrary to the order of chivalry which he professed; and therefore he determined to beg leave of the duke and dutchess, to set out for Saragossa, as the time of the tournament approached; for, there he laid his account with winning the armour which is the reward of the victor. (2,52)

The reference to "scratches" is a tie-back to the cat scratching incident in Chapter 46. The rest of the sentence presents Quixote's intentions for future action, and, in due course, he does set out for Saragossa (2,57) only to have his plans derailed when he discovers that the spurious Quixote has been there ahead of him (2,59). The mention of the tournament at Saragossa is also a tie-back to the very beginning of Volume 2. In Chapter 4, the young bachelor Sampson Carrasco (who, in the guise of the Knight of the White Moon, finally defeats Quixote on the beach at Barcelona) first suggests the plan of competing at Saragossa. Saragossa, we are reminded, is the nominal concrete object of Quixote's wandering through the first 58 chapters of Volume 2. In this way, a fairly innocuous and utilitarian piece of narrative manages to send out threads or tentacles backward and forward across dozens or hundreds of pages. (And I haven't mentioned that in Volume 2, Chapter 4, just before the Saragossa plan comes up, Sancho has been explaining about the miraculous disappearance and appearance of Dapple way back in Volume 1, Chapter 23. I call juxtaposed leaps like this tie-back golf.)

Another variation of the substitute memory or tie-back device is the summary or rehearsal of previous events. In Volume 2, Chapter 62, Quixote and Sancho have arrived in Barcelona and are staying with a wealthy gentleman named Don Antonio Moreno.

> ...and Sancho was ravished with the thoughts of having so luckily found, without knowing how, or wherefore, another wedding of Camacho, another house like that of Don Diego de Miranda, and another palace equal to the duke's castle, where he had been so hospitably entertained. (2,62)

The tentacles here reach back to Don Camacho's wedding in Chapter 20, the sojourn at Don Diego's house in Chapter 18, and the long series of episodes involving the Duke and Duchess beginning in Chapter 30. Here the thread of remembered events is built into the structure of Sancho's character; what he remembers is a series of free meals. A few lines later, in conversation with their host, Sancho is asked about his governorship, and again we get a summary of previous events:

> "Yes, sure, replied the squire; and that of an island called Barataria, which I governed according to my own will and pleasure, for the space of ten days [2, 45-53], during which I lost my natural rest, and learned to despise all the governments upon earth: I, therefore, fled from it, as I would fly from the devil, and tumbled into a cavern [2, 55], from whence, tho' I have myself up as a dead man, I was brought up alive by a perfect miracle [2, 55]."

I won't go on about this; there are dozens of variations of the tie-back device crucial to knitting together a long narrative. And once the reader has them pointed out, he can begin to find them every-

where, though clearly a novel is written so that many of these repetitions work their magic beneath the level of conscious reading.

I won't go on, as I say, though I can't resist mentioning the
lovely little cage/bird-cage motif Cervantes threads through the
book. This begins at the very end of Volume 1 when Quixote
returns home trapped in what he believes is an enchanted cage.
Then a few chapters later (2,6) Quixote tells his niece that if
knightly sentiments didn't completely occupy his attention, he
could make anything, "especially bird-cages and tooth-picks." A
couple of hundred pages later (2,32), he recollects that "I once
found myself cooped up in a cage." Shortly after (2,38), the afflicted
(bearded, transvestite) duenna tells the story of a knight-seducer
who could play the guitar, write poetry, dance and "make bird-
cages." This knight is clearly a graded version of Quixote himself.
The cracked love story the afflicted duenna tells ends with the lovers
enchanted into statues by the malign giant Malumbruno, and it's
Quixote's job to earn their disenchantment, just as he must find a
way to disenchant Dulcinea (that means Quixote is actually two
characters inside the story: the knight-seducer and the redeemer).
The last cage reference in the novel corresponds with Quixote's realization that he will never see Dulcinea just as he and Sancho return
to their home village (2,73). Two boys fighting over a cage of crick-
ets seem like an omen to the old sad knight. Sancho buys the cage
from the boys and hands it to Quixote, hoping to disarm the omen
and dispel his gloom.

The key point to realize is that the novel, the new long narrative form of the book, requires devices like this to keep it from, to
use Nabokov's verb, sprawling. These are forms dictated by the
possibilities of length discovered in the technology of written texts.
And notice also that in this regard form drives content; that is, once
the author realizes the need for substitute-memory devices as the
novel proceeds, then he realizes that chapter openings, dialogue
scenes and character thought will often need tie-backs and summary
rehearsals of earlier material written into them, or he will need to
bring back a character from an earlier incident (creating, perhaps, a
thread or a small subplot, or even a major subplot).

Another thing to notice is the way these substitute-memory devices
relate to character consciousness. The need for substitute-memory

devices puts pressure on the novel to supply more and more of the internal life of characters. Again, what is interesting in *Don Quixote* is to see how Cervantes deploys his substitute memories. Of the four examples I've cited above, one is a description of Quixote's thoughts somewhat distanced by being told through Cid Hamet Benengeli; one is in Sancho's thoughts; and two are in dialogue. The two dialogue examples are more in the style of the drama than the novel; in the drama as in films, the author can't reference a character's interior life except through dialogue, and even then it tends to feel awkward and unnatural. I suspect this is the main reason feature films run mostly between an hour and two hours: films and plays simply can't supply the substitute-memory devices needed to develop length (it has nothing to do with TV and shorter attention spans).

The fact remains that the need for substitute-memory devices, over time, pushed the long story to develop character thought (self-consciousness) as a medium for creating novel memory (or, to put it another way, organic unity, coherence, focus—those things which are the opposite of sprawl). In my previously mentioned essay on novel structure, I wrote about character consciousness and memory-substitute devices in a more general way as novel thought.

These various kinds of thought, their temporal modes (call them recapitulative, grounding and anticipatory), should be in the text, as I say, continuously. Characters should always be connecting events in their own heads (so the reader can remember and see the connection). Every chapter or scene or event or plot step should have some memory or reference to previous chapters, especially the one just before. And every chapter or scene or event or plot step should look ahead, have reference to what's coming up. All these references occur in the point-of-view character's mind, in novel thought. Over and over in novels you'll find a pattern. The chapter opens, then there will be a tiny bit of backfill connecting this chapter or plot step to the last one, maybe a summary of the steps to this point, and a clear sense of what the character plans to get out of the coming scenes. This is followed by the event/scenes. Then, as the chapter closes, you will find a section of reflection on

141

what has just happened and a moment of decision or plan-making—Where do I turn next? A novel is always making connections within itself. ("Notes on Novel Structure" *The New Quarterly*, Number 87)

This device also makes possible a new conception of character based not on adherence to abstract moral concepts (honour, chastity, filial piety, feudal loyalty) but on the accumulation of particular memories. Sancho's summary rehearsal of events in the novel is different from Quixote's. Actually, Quixote hews to a more primitive concept of character construction: he has no memory, except for books, and his reasons for doing things come from outside the novel. For example, look at "thought" from an earlier romance, Gottfried von Strassburg's *Tristan and Isolt*:

> When Tristan felt the pangs of Love, then he bethought him straightway of his faith and honor, and would fain have set himself free. "Nay," he said to himself, "let such things be, Tristan; guard thee well, lest others perceive thy thoughts." So would he turn his own heart, fighting against his own will, and desiring against his own desire....
> (*Medieval Romances,* Loomis, Ed., 162)

And here is a bit from *Sir Gawain and the Green Knight*:

> It would have been a perilous time for both of them, if Mary had not taken thought for her knight. For that noble princess urged him so, and pressed him so hard to confess himself her lover, that at last he must needs either accept her love or bluntly refuse her. And he was troubled for his courtesy, for fear that he should behave like a churl, but more afraid of a wound to his honor, if he behaved badly to his host, the lord of the castle. And that at any rate, he said to himself, should not happen. So he laughed a little, though kindly, and put aside all the fond loving words that sprang to his lips. (*Medieval Romances,* 370)

These moments of thought, dramatic in themselves, are static in terms of temporal reach; they do nothing to gather the narrative, as it were, into itself. And the characters they construct, as a consequence, are rather flat and abstract.

As a result of this contrast in the way Sancho and Quixote think, we end up knowing more about Sancho than Quixote, and Sancho ends up knowing himself. This, I suspect, is a major turning point in the development of the novel in general. Cervantes has constructed Sancho and Quixote as parallel characters. Quixote wants Dulcinea, Sancho wants an island to govern. They are both the victims of illusions and hoaxes. But after ten days of governing the island of Barataria, Sancho resigns the office. Why? Because he knows who he is and this governing business isn't him. And the way he couches his resignation is in terms of a contrast between his present and former life, that is, with memories of his former life. In the contrast, he finds himself. It's a gorgeous passage, gently comic but also one of the most touching moments in the novel; it begins with Sancho silently walking down to the stable and embracing Dapple, his donkey.

> "Come hither, my dear companion! my friend, and sharer of all my toils and distress; when you and I consorted together, and I was plagued with no other thoughts than the care and mending of your furniture, and pampering your little body, happy were my hours, my days, and my years! but, since I quitted you and mounted on the towers of pride and ambition, my soul has been invaded by a thousand miseries...." (2,53)

Sancho harnesses Dapple and prepares to leave, then turning to his advisers and courtiers, he makes his formal disavowal of office.

> "...I was not born to be governor, or to defend islands and cities from the assaults of their enemies: I am better versed in ploughing and delving, in pruning and planting vines, than enacting laws, and defending provinces and kingdoms...." (2,53)

It's precisely at this point that Sancho invents a concept of self that is nowhere else evident in the novel, a self based on personal experience and forged in the arena of self-education through the correction of desire. Throughout the novel, Sancho has let Quixote be his guide; Quixote infects him with the desire for an island to govern and for power. But at the testing place, Sancho reaches into himself, into memory, and asserts his individuality. He renounces the dream and inverts the quest (literally): "..let me return to my ancient liberty; let me go in quest of my former life, that I may enjoy a resurrection from this present death." (2,53) From this point forward, the emphasis of the novel in general will move progressively inward, into the mental and emotional life of its characters; the outer quest will be replaced by the inner quest. By contrast, we never actually know what Quixote thinks after his defeat by the Knight of the White Moon or why he suddenly becomes sane at the very end and reverts to his former name. A kind of self is being born here, too; but Quixote is a self because of his persistence in being, his compulsive madness, while Sancho is a self because he has remembered who he is.

This is only a sketch, but it's fascinating to speculate that in solving a technical problem related to length, novelists also were beginning to invent psychology, which I take to be the modern science of mental structures based on the accumulation of personal history.

The Reader Theme

One very ingenious substitute memory device is what I call the reader theme. In producing a sequel to Volume 1, Cervantes faced the daunting task of publishing a second book ten years after the first that would yet extend the structure of the first in such a way as to make the two books into an organic whole. This is a variation of the problem of length. The easiest solution is simply to have Quixote break out again, which is what Cervantes does (in the chronology of the novel, only a month has passed since he returned home in that enchanted cage). But Cervantes seems to have realized this simple repetition (the third break-out) might seem thin and pale without some significant variation and the addition of devices of coherence. This is, of course, the usual problem with add-on stories and sequels.

So he hit upon the reader theme strategy as a way of integrating the first part of *Don Quixote* into the second part. As Volume 2 opens, the first part has just been published with a huge popular success, according to Sampson Carrasco, who reports:

> "...the very children handle it, boys read it, men understand, and old people applaud it: in short, it is so thumbed, so read, and so well known by everybody, that no sooner a meager horse appears, than they say, 'There goes Rozinante;' but those who peruse it most, are your pages: you cannot go into a nobleman's antichamber, where you won't find a Don Quixote, which is no sooner laid down by one, than another takes it up, some struggling, and some intreating for a sight of it...." (2,3)

(The fact that it seems to have taken only a month for the first part of *Don Quixote* to get written, printed and achieve widespread distribution wreaks havoc with verisimilitude; strict realist critics like to point to elements like this as examples of Cervantes' carelessness, whereas it is obviously a joke and evidence that Cervantes thought of his book as a literary confection and not an imitation of reality in any superficial sense.) As Volume 2 develops, Quixote meets reader after reader who is familiar with the first part. The reason the Duke and Duchess can so thoroughly hoodwink him is that, as readers, they are privy to his most personal thoughts, fancies and memories from Volume 1. They know him as well as the reader of the novel knows him, better than he knows himself, which is a state of affairs no real human being ever suffers, only characters in books.

> As they had read the first part of the history, from which they had learned the extravagant humour of Don Quixote, they waited with infinite pleasure, and the most eager desire of being acquainted with the original, fully determined to gratify his humour in every thing, and treat him all the time he should stay with them, as a real knight-errant; that is, with all the ceremonies described in those books of chivalry they had read, and to which, indeed, they were greatly attached. (2,30)

The reader theme uses the publication of Volume 1 as a substitute memory device that periodically holds that first book up to the mind's eye and keeps it present (a shadow book) continually throughout Quixote's new adventures. This is obvious from the way Cervantes uses Carrasco to summarize the signal events of Volume I:

> "No, sure, replied the knight; but tell me Mr. batchelor, which of my exploits is most esteemed in this history?" "As to that particular, said the batchelor, there are as many different opinions as there are different tastes. Some stick to the adventure of the windmills, which to your worship appeared monstrous giants; others, to that of the fulling-mills; this reader, to the description of the two armies, which were afterwards metamorphosed into flocks of sheep; while another magnifies that of the dead body, which was carrying to the place of interment in Segovia: one says, that the deliverance of the galley-slaves excels all the rest; and a second affirms, that none of them equals the adventure of the Benedictine giants, and your battle with the valiant Biscayner." Here Sancho interrupting him again, said, "Tell me, Mr. batchelor, is the adventure of the Yanguesians mentioned, when our modest Rozinante longed for green pease in December." "Nothing, replied Sampson, has escaped the pen of the sage author, who relates everything most minutely, even the capers which honest Sancho cut in the blanket." "I cut no capers in the blanket, answered Sancho: but in the air, I grant you, I performed more than I desired." (2,3)

This is a rehearsal of Volume I, an example of the reader theme being used as a substitute memory device just as we earlier saw Cervantes using rehearsals and tie-backs in his chapter openings.

But having set the device in motion, Cervantes, who is a genius at the elaboration of form, must have realized how useful it would be for him to extend the reader theme throughout the remainder of the novel. In a word, he floods the zone with news of Volume I, creating jokes, echoes, and even structural modifications: the reader theme creates motivation (for the hoaxes as well as certain compositional changes in the structure of the novel itself) and creates content (the style and substance of the hoaxes). The reader theme blossoms, shifts gears and becomes central to plot and meaning. In effect, the whole enterprise of the second volume acquires a certain metafictional spin which only increases with the addition of the spurious second volume (the nudge) and another set of characters and readers. For example, when the old don reaches Barcelona, richly caparisoned riders who have read both Volume 1 and the false sequel gallop out to meet him, exclaiming,

> "Welcome to our city, thou mirrour, lanthorn, planet, and polar star of all chivalry in its utmost extent! welcome, valorous Don Quixote de la Mancha, not the false, ficti-tious, and apocryphal adventurer, lately in spurious history described; but, the real, legal, and loyal knight recorded by Cid Hamet Benengeli, the flower of historians." (2,61)

The fact that the first volume has just been published inspires Quixote and Sancho to break out again because they see themselves suddenly as the subject of a book, characters with a responsibility to provide story for their chronicler. Talking to student Carrasco, it is Quixote who broaches the subject of a second part.

> "And pray, resumed Don Quixote, does the author promise a second part?" "Yes, said Sampson, but, he says, he has not yet found it,...." (2,4)

To which Sancho replies:

> "...I would have Mr. Moor take care, and consider what he is about; for, my master and I will furnish him with mate-rials, in point of adventures and different events, sufficient to compose not only one, but an hundred second parts...if my master had taken my advice, we might have already been in the fields, redressing grievances, and righting wrongs, according to the use and custom of knights-errant." (2,4)

Sancho's enthusiasm is comic and spontaneous whereas Quixote's own first reaction to being written about is anxious. For not only is he haunted by that spurious sequel to Volume 1 and the doubles of himself and Sancho who precede him to Saragossa, he is haunted by himself in that earlier book. He is the first hero in fic-tion to suffer from an uncanny awareness, however indirect and inexpressible (he can only think of it in terms of enchanters), that he is a character in a book.

"...and when I went to welcome him, he told me there was a printed book about your worship's history, in which you go by the name of 'the ingenious squire Don Quixote de la Mancha;' and that I am mentioned in it, by my own name of Sancho Panza, as well as my lady Dulcinea del Toboso, with other things that passed between you and me only; at hearing of which, I crossed myself through fear, wondring, how they should come to the knowledge of the historian."

"You may depend upon it, Sancho, said Don Quixote, the author of our history must be some sage enchanter; for nothing is hid from writers of that class." (2,2)

NIGHT THOUGHTS OF AN INSOMNIAC READER, OR THEMATIC MEDITATIONS

...I am fond of reading even the torn scraps of paper in the streets.... (1,9)

Why Books Are to Blame

Reading has often been viewed as a suspiciously solitary pursuit variously connected with a multitude of modern developments from the rise of the individual to protestant Christianity, masturbation, and, in Don Quixote's case, insanity. In part, this has something to do with two social trends attributable to the invention of books: the democratization of access to texts and the increased privacy of the individual reader in relation to the book he is reading. As soon as a book moves into the public domain, the author or the powers that be lose control of its transmission and also of its meaning. As Henri-Jean Martin observes in his book *The History and Power of Writing*, even

> Luther himself wondered whether he had been right to translate the Bible and put it into the hands of readers who drew conclusions that he condemned. (*The History and Power of Writing*, 228)

A precisely parallel technological revolution has been taking place over the past twenty years in regard to the Internet which is variously seen as tool of liberal democracy and an ungovernable conduit for pornography. Some people become so attached to the new technology that they have to be treated for Internet addiction, a circumstance that can only remind us of Alonso Quixano's addiction to chivalric romances.

> ...this said honest gentleman, at his leisure hours, which engrossed the greater part of the year, addicted himself to the reading of books of chivalry, which he perused with such rapture and application, that he not only forgot the pleasures of the chace, but also utterly neglected the management of his estate: nay to such a pass did his curiosity and madness, in this particular, drive him, that he sold many good acres of Terra Firma, to purchase books.... (1,1)

Books (and the Internet) degrade social control and cohesiveness by allowing freer access to ideas, many of which have a libidinal accent, and by seducing the individual into communion with a fantasmal, non-human, anti-social interface.

The change from orality to literacy alters the role of memory in human life, changes social structure, changes modes of knowing, changes consciousness itself and our experience of time. In an oral culture, the self is defined within a relatively small network of human relations—family, clan, moiety, band, tribe. It fits as a place taker in a structured social system and matures through a series of ritual life stages and initiations based on myth and orally transmitted wisdom. Everyone's life repeats the same story. Knowledge resides in and is limited by biological memory, and the social structure functions both as a network of individual memories and as a mnemonic device itself (social structure repeats mythic structure which in turn repeats the structure of relations among the flora and fauna in a system of parallel hierarchical structures).

As soon as you introduce writing (and books), the locus of consciousness begins to shift subtly away from dependence on biological memory and the human network of oral culture. In a literate culture, my memory has a much smaller role in my interaction with the world. Rather than rely on memory, I need to know how to access information in a library or on the Internet. Knowing how to read, that is, knowing how to access books as databases becomes more important than being able to remember facts or give facts a moral resonance (what we call wisdom). That skill is very impersonal and subverts and diminishes, to an extent, my merely personal memories. The self, without memory, becomes an assembly point for information, which, once assembled, packaged and used, can be forgotten.

The books themselves link to other books creating a nearly endless non-human network of memory storage devices. The human basis of knowledge (traditional wisdom) begins to evaporate as does the need for the organized social relations of an oral culture. In a sense, the new mind gives itself up to the book; books talk to each other through us; our lives no longer mime identical stories inside the social structure; we have become temporary, reusable conduits for books. This is a crucial moment in human history when the self, the individual, makes its first appearance and simultaneously begins to empty itself of substance. The modern self becomes less an entity than a media reader.

That's what we are in this world, the given of selfhood. But this giving up of the self to books makes us uneasy. We worry anxiously about those parts of ourselves being constructed by language, by books; in this sense, contemporary theory mirrors back to us the way the self actually does function in a literate universe. We worry about those "gaps" and the parts of ourselves that are not accessible by books: dreams, the unconscious, which we analogize as texts—interminable texts which rarely give up their secrets. Not to mention all those disconnected fragments of pre-bookish, even pre-linguistic, snippets of cultural DNA, messages from the deep past. All of which contributes to our experience of insubstantiality, fleetingness and relativity. In the world of the book, the self and the world share the labyrinthine slipperiness of language.

In a sense, books read us. Books require a kind of passive handing over of mental authority to the book itself. As Merlin Donald says,

> This is more than a metaphor; each time the brain carries out an operation in concert with the external symbolic storage system [e.g. a book], it becomes part of a network. Its memory structure is temporarily altered; and the locus of cognitive control changes. (*Origins of the Modern Mind*, 312)

Without the advantage of computer network and hardware systems as an analytical metaphor, Cervantes focuses here on the role of imagination in the parallel processes of reading and perception. While we read, the words of the book thread through us, inspiring imaginative reconstructions of what the text describes; these reconstructions are the next thing to experience itself, easily mistaken for the real thing. Verisimilitude, literary realism, is a dangerous lie.

Cervantes' narrator ostensibly writes the whole novel as an indictment of those chivalric romances that mislead and corrupt readers with their shallow untruths and drive Quixote insane. In *Eros the Bittersweet*, Anne Carson suggests that texts themselves are erotic, that is, they inspire desire, because both desire and metaphor share an imaginative core. In Volume 2, as part of a hoax perpetrated on Quixote by the Duke and Duchess, the afflicted (she has a beard) duenna tells the story of a pair of enchanted lovers (2,38) misled by the erotic sentiments of lyric poetry. The duenna even cites Plato, whose famous condemnation of poets in the *Republic* is clearly at the heart of her argument.

"...seeing the mischief that hath befallen me, thro' these and other verses, I have often thought, that wise and well-regulated commonwealths ought to expel the poets, according to the advice of Plato; at least your lascivious writers who compose couplets, not like those of the marquiss of Mantua, that entertain and draw tears from women and children...they [poems] produce a kind of palpitation in the soul, a titillation of good humour, an agitation in the nerves, and finally, a tremulous motion, like that of quicksilver in all the senses. Therefore, I repeat it to this honourable company, that such dangerous rhymers ought to be banished to the isle of Lizzards: yet, they are not so much to blame, as the simple wretches who applaud, and the boobies who believe them...." (2,38)

All the anti-romance arguments in *Don Quixote* can be read ironically, but this one most of all. The speaker is a man with a beard posing as a woman, an enchanted duenna. His story has been concocted from elements of Quixote's own narrative by the Duke and Duchess who have read Volume 1. The argument against poetry is clearly meant to be read with tongue in cheek, and, by implication, all the other arguments against romance novels elsewhere in the book.

Plato's attack on poets ironically filtered through the lips of the cross-dressing, bearded duenna renders the effect of reading poetry as something very like sexual arousal. Cervantes is playing a game here with the ideas of titillation and text and the paradoxical notion that while you are reading you are not yourself, that in reading we somehow allow the books to read us. In this sense, the book is an external memory device that subtly diminishes the sovereignty of the individual over his own mental processes, and *Don Quixote* can be read as a tract on the effect of books on the self. When a reader goes "on line" and "accesses" the stored data in a book, he gives up reliance on his own memory and becomes something other than himself. Being played by a book, as Cervantes tells us, is a form of temporary insanity.

This notion is at once about language itself (a matter of logic and definitions, as it were) and a matter of psychological insight. The imagination has the ability to generate images, scenarios, stories and ideas, but in reading it gives itself over to the book. In a sense, the book generates the images in the imagination which acts, as I say, something like a media player. The imagination's reconstruction of the book is a fiction, which nonetheless has the feel of reality because the imagination—this is crucial—plays a similar role in constructing pictures of reality.

In reading we play with distance. We are simultaneously inside the reality of the book and outside it, sitting in an armchair with a book in hand—that flickering quality again. The danger comes from identifying too closely with the reality of the book as Quixote does. He imagines himself into *Amadis of Gaul* so thoroughly that his thoughts and actions no longer fit in the outside world. This inappropriateness of act and thought to setting is what Cervantes calls Quixote's madness. The absurd story of the bearded duenna runs parallel since she (he) mistakes the erotic (masturbatory) physical sensations inspired by poetry for love. Reading poetry is almost like being in love. Lacan might say it is the same as being in love, given the imaginary nature of reality and relationships.

Don Quixote is less about knights-errant than it is about books. It's about the New World of books in which memory and consciousness somehow float, belong not to me or my body but elsewhere. The pathos of literacy lies in the disruption of reality, not what it is but how we experience it. The invention of letters, text and books disrupted the oral-mythic experience of reality and replaced it with something else, call it theory. Caught in the middle, Quixote compulsively consults fake oracles (Mr. Peter's ape and the talking head), but he also visits a printing shop and talks about the theory of translation. This is the house of the new metaphysics.

Yet vestiges and remnants of the old experience of meaning persist; our feeling of not being quite real, being constructed or mediated, exists against the ground of an alternative view, indistinctly recalled, romanticized and sentimentalized at the level of the demotic. Rousseau's myth of the Noble Savage, for example, still animates the popular imagination and mediates our attempts to find truth other than a bookish truth in everything from organic vegetables to natural fibres, exercise regimes and camping trips, just as Plato's attempt to turn myth into theory created a well-worn groove that haunts contemporary discourse. Instead of talking about the world of appearances and the world of reality, we talk about language creating meaning, about the imaginary and the real.

Quixote, who is equally able to talk literary criticism and to believe the false jargon of book-learned knight-errantry, is the quintessential modern, the first modern man. Sancho, though illiterate, is modern, too—the Wal-Mart version, a bag of fragmentary folk-wisdom, shallow as a plate, lacking the dignity and context of a mythic meta-story. Cervantes was quite clear that illiteracy does not equate with orality. Sancho's proverbs and apophthegms are the illiterate version of the fractured and impoverished discourses of the ancients, the stories from the time before time.

When, at the Duke's dinner table, Quixote takes the priest to task for mere book-learning, a bookworm "who never entered or trod the paths of chivalry," we must not see the sentiment as merely an ironic anti-intellectual reaction. It is a very old sentence, a voice from the age of oral lore mounting the echo of a protest against the coming of the new, which marks it for destruction. Quixote himself is the expert, the book-learned arbiter of all things chivalric in the novel, except that he never trained, never practiced, never suffered and never met a knight first-hand in his life.

It's not simply that the age of knight-errantry has passed; it's that the chain of human memory through which the lore, laws and customs of knight-errantry were passed down from mythic times has been broken. The pathos of literacy is not just that Quixote reads books and goes mad; it's the fact that all that remains of an ancient tradition, a truth, is garbled versions of old stories written down in books. The first characteristic of modernity is the quality of what it has forgotten. Quixote wants to undergo a spiritual quest without knowing anything but the Hollywood version. Or as Denis de Rougement writes in *Love in the Western World*, "...the character of Don Quixote was ridiculous only because he wished to undergo an *askesis* for which he had not received initiation." (*Love in the Western World*, 189) Here the idea of "initiation" is synonymous with the ritual aspect of oral transmission.

Books swept away whole cultures even as curious writers took notes, so that all we have are the notes, fragments of quotations. Books begin by subverting the importance of human memory. They are memory storage devices which by sheer extensiveness and resistance to change are superior to memory. Those who knew the tribal truths and passed them on to initiates lost their power as well as their secrets to the books, and the knowledge that was once private became public. Information replaced wisdom; science replaced myth. And the myths that once organized whole societies degenerated into legend and folklore and fodder for novelists who seek to exploit their aura of ancient knowledge which, by an odd, romantic transposition, seems more real, closer to nature, closer to God, than anything our current information age can provide.

I do not mean that the discourse of myth is either inferior or superior to the discourse of theory, that oral stories are somehow less or more real than novels published as books. But memory is so tied into our idea of personal identity that what is forgotten comes to represent to us an image of lost self, lost essence. What we have forgotten begins to *feel* more real than the information we can look up in the library.

To be modern is to be haunted by what we have lost, that is the spirit of romanticism, which is our style of yearning for an unreachable past (read: Dulcinea). So that the past itself becomes an object of desire, and the book that created the breach in the chain of transmission, that is, created the gap of desire, situates itself in the gap. In books we try to write our way across a chasm toward some impossibly happy conclusion, a wholeness that is beyond time and unforgettable. But the book, in its archival aspect, only reminds us of our fallibility, or purely human forgetfulness, the impossibility of remembering everything.

For contemporary Euro-moderns, the wrench is long past, though the old sentences still filter through us (the teenager's contempt for what only appears in books). Even the urbane Plato sometimes looks quaint struggling to fudge those ancient stories into something resembling theory. But we have been spectators for centuries as other oral cultures go down before us. For them, the pathos of literacy is a living experience.

Books replaced the religious, educational and epistemological framework of orality by interrupting the chain of oral transmission, the role of ordinary human memory and the authority of poets, shamans and wise elders and replaced it with mere book-learning. In Euro-Western history, this happened twice: the first time in

Classical Greece and the second time in Western Europe during the Middle Ages. Plato dramatized the onset of the first revolutionary transformation from orality to literacy in the *Phaedrus* where he has Socrates deliver a fable about the invention of writing in ancient Egypt. When Theuth, the ibis-god, shows King Thamus his new art, the king replies:

> ...this discovery of yours will create forgetfulness in the learners' souls, because they will not use their memories; they will trust to the external written characters and not remember of themselves.

The new book-learning not only inspires forgetfulness, but it alters the oral system of traditional wisdom, the role of authority and the educational system on which it is based.

> As for wisdom [says Thamus], it is the reputation, not the reality, that you have to offer to those who learn from you; they will have heard many things and yet received no teaching; they will appear to be omniscient and will generally know nothing....

Not only does the role of memory, self, community, and education change, but as soon as we begin storing memory in more or less permanent external devices, certain crucial definitions begin to change. In an oral culture, truth tends to be defined pragmatically (the buffalo is on the other side of the hill: go and shoot it) and by authority or tradition (what the wise men say). But writing changes the definition of truth. Over time a written or printed statement can be compared with other statements (critical thinking), and a statement can be compared with experiential reality in a more thoroughgoing way. We can invent experiments; science follows. We can track far more complex sequences of deductions to arrive at truths derived from previous truths. And finally there are new truths based on definitions and changing definitions of words (something that is extremely difficult to track orally).

These changes in definition, like the changes in the locus of memory and the changes in the way we represent the world to ourselves also become objects of representation themselves. As the locus of modern memory has shifted away from its biological root, the mind has increasingly begun to think about its own representational processes, that is, we have invented theory, linguistic philosophy, hermeneutics, literary criticism, etc. as ways of coming to grips with our own new modes of thought. In other words, one of the effects of books, of the transformation of human culture from orality to literacy is the invention of, well, literary theory. As Merlin Donald writes in *Origins of the Modern Mind*,

> Metalinguistic skills have been essential to human success with the ESS system [external symbolic system] and have been the core of educational curricula for two millennia, starting with classical rhetoric and moving through various additional stages. The curricular focus has moved from speech to script; from overall narrative structure to the intricate thought skills embedded in grammar, logic, and induction; and from extended narrative model building to the construction of increasingly specialized theoretic products. (*Origins of the Modern Mind*, 358)

Thus when Plato has Thamus say that books create the "reputation" of wisdom and not the "reality," he is offering a theoretical argument from the point of view of an oral culture in flux, a culture in which two definitions of wisdom operate. And since the transformation from orality to literacy didn't happen overnight (it is still going on), arguments like this tend to thread through the history of thought without ever actually disappearing. Not only do earlier modes of consciousness (mythic, oral) as well as literary forms (e.g. the tropes, schemes and devices of classical rhetoric) persist within even literate cultures, but the old truths and definitions of truth still fight a kind of rearguard action against modernity and postmodernity. We still find ourselves yearning for what, to our nostalgia-ridden souls, seemed like a Golden Age of epic poetry and heroic, self-sustaining selfhood.

> "Happy age, and happy days were those, to which the ancients gave the name of golden; not, that gold, which in these iron-times is so much esteemed, was to be acquired without trouble, in that fortunate period; but, because people then, were ignorant of those two words MINE and THINE: in that sacred age, all things were in common...."
> (1,11)

Cervantes, who lived in a world of burgeoning though still hardly universal literacy (and bourgeois economic concerns), just a century and bit after the invention of printing, was perfectly aware of the revolutionary changes taking place in Europe. Books and writing had almost disappeared from the landscape after the fall of Rome; the literacy revolution had to reconquer old territory during the Middle Ages, and Spain, the Arab beachhead on the continent, with its huge libraries, was a primary source for the reintroduction of the book. Not only that, but the recent conquests in America had revealed vast, complex oral societies in Mexico and Peru. Finding himself in a swirl of what Merlin Donald calls "cognitive vestiges," oral remnants, old arguments, traditional claims and the new claims of the world of literacy (which seem to us today still startlingly fresh), Cervantes, instead of taking a position, takes every position. By running his characters through a series of actions, he interrogates the nature of the new forms of representation, of books. That is, he does theory. But since he is doing it by writing a novel, he doesn't advance a theory. Rather, he deploys a set of arguments and counter-arguments (in dialogue and reflection), ironic paradoxes, and exemplary images (of character action and plot) around the nature of books, reading, truth, imitation, imagination and reality.

In *Don Quixote*, Cervantes captures one of the signal moments in the history of human evolution like a prehistoric bug in amber. Looking back nostalgically, Quixote tries to enter a myth by reading about it in a book. But the book mangles the myth; it cannot *translate* the language of myth into the language of books because the language of myth depends upon a certain technology of transmission and retention. The medium does change the message. Quixote does everything wrong; he marches under the sign of inappropriateness; and the fragmentary elements of myth emerge in the text willy-nilly, at random, like dream images. But once the skein of oral transmission, initiation and memory has been severed, once you have given the self over to the book, then a whole new world of worry opens up. First you want to write a book, then to be written up in a book (the invention of celebrity), and then you realize that anyone can write your story, that some hack might just write an erroneous version as convincing to readers as the truth. Truth and identity go out the window, and you resort to begging testimonials from strangers at wayside inns. And you are a mark and a victim for every reader who has read the book and thus is privy to the nuance of your innermost thoughts. Indeed, the reader knows you better than you know yourself since you've already started to forget and maybe you've been lying to yourself all along.

Novels are tales of suffering for love, but "love" is here a multiple signifier—it becomes a metaphor for all yearning and desire. In the contemporary parlance, the self is encircled by gaps; there isn't just one abyss, they are multiple, as common as potholes. And they communicate or resonate by a kind of inter-play of metaphor, analogy, parallelism, and cross-reference; my emptiness with your emptiness; creating by repetition the textural simulacra of meaning and truth: love, desire, book, sign, metaphor, truth—words that map absence rather than substance. It's fascinating that after all the beatings and disappointments Quixote remains impervious to reason. If *Don Quixote* were merely about appearance and reality, then reality would at some point flood the gap of desire with meaning; what my creative writing students call an epiphany would occur. But so-called reality never convinces Quixote of anything, least of all that Dulcinea is an illusion. It takes another sign, an omen, to make him recognize he will never see her. "Malum Signum, Malum Signum! the hare flies, the hounds pursue, and Dulcinea does not appear."

Don Quixote mimes the loss (desire) created by the invention of the book. It deploys a dual metonymy; Quixote wants to be a knight-errant and a knight-errant is always in love with an impossible object. His essence is a paradox. Quixote's inspiration derives from romance novels, which manipulate the fragmentary remnants of oral myths as their narrative furniture. The novel instantiates the knight's quest and the ideal of chaste love as a metaphor for the quest for forgotten being and finds inside itself its own subject, how love is always destroying the thing it loves just as we disrupt the chain of oral transmission, the world of myth, as soon as we try to preserve it in books.

On a certain level, *Don Quixote* is what it says it is, an anti-book, a novel against all novels (call them what you will: chivalric romances or tales of suffering for love). The world of dream and myth exacts its revenge and puts a stop to the folly in the person of the Knight of the White Moon. And when the spurious Don

Quixote walks out of the pages of his book into the pages of our book, the book itself becomes an impossible text, an image of the mystery and paradox of life itself.

Character and Symptom

Coincident with literacy and the advent of bookish consciousness, it has become an intellectual shibboleth to think of reality and the self as more or less socially or linguistically constructed entities. The book erodes the traditional sense of self as a monad in a social system, with a substantial role as carrier of a portion of the group memory. In modern Euro-Western culture, the self becomes a conduit, an emptiness, that functions only insofar as it plugs into the network (this is the larger meaning and threat of globalism). Walter Benjamin talks about the diminishing importance of experience in the information world, which is to say that personal experience and personal history are far less significant to the modern self than the contentless ability to access facts on a database. What we *know* is a set of culturally transmitted messages and access codes wrapped around the gaping hole of desire. Imagination and imitation create a shimmering screen of imagined selves and imitated others. Naturally, we tend to go around feeling slightly anxious and irritated about this (the common sense reaction to theory). And what is really real, as Lacan says, only impinges in a kind of accidental way. When this happens, we view it as traumatic—nothing like what we expected; take death (or the current war in Iraq), for example.

The old philosophies and metaphysics—say, Kant, who reworked Plato to make him modern—are next thing to voodoo (even Lacan can't escape the taint of dualism). The new philosophies debate the meaning of words, texts become the only dependable reality worth investigating. We live in a world of so-called information technology yet seem to know less and less about what is real in our hearts; postmodern life skills increasingly revolve around knowing how to access databases. In his madness (you have to be a bit insane to ask what is real), naïveté and ignorance, Quixote attempts to become the last great European shaman, suffering, fighting his way across the chasm toward the mystic light. "Come along with me," he says to the murderous dandy Roque Guinart (2,60),

> and learn to be a knight-errant, in which capacity you will undergo such toils and disasters as will be deemed suffi- cient penance, and exalt you to heaven in the turning of two balls.

The light's name is Dulcinea, and Quixote is a flop as a knight- errant and shaman (also extremely irritable, violent and melancholy for a Christian saint).

Every effort at representation is logically bound to fail when it is measured against identity. The picture we construct will never be the thing itself. This representational or mimetic paradox is so central to Western thought that the cunning and witty Borges made it the theme of his story "Pierre Menard, Author of the Quixote" in which a twentieth century author sets out to rewrite *Don Quixote*, word for word, from scratch, not copying it, but recreating it exactly. The paradox presented in the story is that, somehow, this new *Don Quixote* will be an improvement on the first, though identical to it, because Menard will have composed it ex nihilo, as it were, without the advantage of having lived Cervantes' life or thought his thoughts. Comparatively speaking, it was easy for Cervantes to write the novel whereas if Menard can reproduce even a few pages it will be "astonishing."

In Borges' short story the original *Don Quixote* stands for reality, on a level with, as Menard writes, "The final term in a theological or metaphysical demonstration—the objective world, God, causal- ity, the forms of the universe...." And his project is to reconstitute that reality as itself—not copy it but to render it as itself. The paradox is that, as Menard observes, "I should have to be immortal to carry it out." That is, the epistemological dream (the realist's dream) of knowing or re-presenting the thing itself (I am trying not to fall into Kantian jargon here) is impossible.

In a very Borgesian moment, Cervantes, himself, has Quixote make precisely the same claim in the context of his imitation of Amadis' lunacy during his sojourn in the Sierra Morena in Volume I.

"This is the point, answered Don Quixote, and refinement of my design: a knight who turns madman, because he cannot help it, can claim no merit for his misfortune; but, the great matter is, to run distracted without cause.... Wherefore, friend Sancho, you need not throw away your time unprofitably, in advising me to refrain from an imitation at once so admirable, rare and happy...." (1,25)

In other words, it's easy to act crazy if you are really crazy but acting crazy when you're sane is an act of creation, of art, and therefore worthy of special merit. The catch or paradox is that Quixote is insane; he's an insane man pretending to be insane. This is the mimetic paradox in a typical Cervantian nutshell: turning knight-errant and falling in love with Dulcinea del Toboso, like the act of representation or consciousness itself (not to mention writing a novel), is a bizarre and lunatic endeavour.

The pathos of mimesis is only one instance of a series of gaps, or rather terms indicating a relation of separation between an intention (desire plus imagined object) and a notionally real object. Logos, language, metaphor, appearance, fancy, mimesis, desire, and love all possess an inherently similar structure defined by separateness or distance or obstacle. The gaps are inscribed with pathos, suffering and story. These concepts aren't exactly interchangeable; they are not synonyms; though, in theory, they share a common referent (that gap), the objectless object, or simply the silence beyond words, the silence of being itself, or, by the logic of verbal substitution, perhaps death. But they seem to vibrate with one another as analogies, the one adding to our conception of the other. The human heart is, it seems, encircled by this chain of analogies or simulacra, by silence and the faux drapery of fantasy. (One can think of this self as a kind of imaginary doughnut, empty inside and outside.)

On one level, the sequence of psychological events that leads to Quixote's mad career is a commonplace of human love. He sees something in a girl, Aldonza Lorenzo, that triggers his infatuation—Cervantes is specific: she's hale and buxom; her breasts become the metonymic trigger of the old man's desire. But she's too far away in all respects: young, lower class, real. He can't bring himself to speak to her. In his fantasy, mediated by the stories of chivalry, he reinvents her as Dulcinea, the paragon. He also reinvents himself as a knight, which he's not. The unreal then tries to have a relationship with the unreal; this is the essence of infatuation, of falling in love, of love at first sight. Quixote both pursues and postpones the inevitable confrontation with whatever constitutes reality in a situation like this by interposing the mimed love rituals of chivalric courtesy which enjoins absence (the road trip and adventures) and chastity. And then, instead of reality, he meets only another sign. As Lacan says, for humans, the only possible sex act is masturbation; and masturbation is to love what solipsism is to philosophy.

This is, one notes in passing, an awfully melancholy yet seductively romantic vision. Literary theory itself sometimes smacks of academic romanticism and intellectual posing. All that truly heroic agonizing over the slipperiness of language at Yale, Duke and the Sorbonne! But it also explains why literary theory has to a large extent colonized philosophy and English departments at colleges and universities in North America. The novel, or perhaps narrative art in general, has become the apex of a philosophical (read theoretical) debate because it encapsulates the paradox of language itself. It is the prototypical instance of a discourse or language game in which truth is determined by coherence, that is, how a statement fits or coheres within a system of statements rather than by reference to an external reality. It makes no sense to try to prove whether Sancho is fat or thin by looking for a peasant named Sancho outside *Don Quixote* itself. The only way to decide if the statement "Sancho is fat" is true is by looking at other sentences in the novel. And this is something like the way we have come to view language itself, as a system of utterances that make sense, gather meaning, only by reference to other utterances within the system while maintaining an, at best, hypothetical relation to some external reality.

Or, to put it slightly differently, a novel is somehow meant to be read as representational (realistic), symbolic (allegorical) and fictional (imaginary) all at once; at the same time, novel form (the surging repetitions of desire and resistance, the reflective parallel structures of subplot and set-piece, the substitute memory devices) is like a grammar that organizes meaning without itself meaning anything (these are the "nonrepresentational" elements referred to by Frye). Whenever we construe the meaning of a sentence (or a novel) there is always something else left over which we have not and possibly cannot take into account. This is a fascinating recognition; it's metaphorically like the dark matter we now suspect makes up most of the substance of the universe though we have no idea where it is or what it does.

Because it's so self-conscious about its own paradoxical bookishness, a novel like *Don Quixote* begs and complicates and thwarts all the usual questions of aboutness. It's about everything that is in it (and being, as Frye says, something of an anatomy, it seems to be about everything): the story of Alonso Quixano going mad and turning into Don Quixote, Alonso's twelve-year infatuation with Aldonza Lorenzo, Don Quixote's chaste, impossible love for Dulcinea del Toboso, Sancho Panza's companionship and his dream of governing an island, the counter-quest of the curate, the barber and the student Carrasco who set out to mimic Quixote's chivalrous fancies and bring him home, the evils of romance novels, the logic of bookish reality (readers, "real" fictional characters, and spurious doubles). It's also about all the subjects dealt with in the various speeches and dialogues, as well as the inset stories, interpolated texts and threaded stories.

It's about the contrast between Quixote and Sancho, the one a chaste lover of an ideal woman who doesn't exist, the other married to a jealous and noisy, if loving, wife; the one lost in the florid discourse of those perfervid romance novels, the other describing his world in an endless flow of banal and cheesy folk wisdom; the one self-destructively heroic, the other mainly interested in staying clear of trouble. It's about all the inter-textual references, the list of medieval romances, the legends, the mythic motifs woven into the action of the book. It's about enchantment, giants and necromancers. It's about Mexico, the Inquisition and the Expulsion of the Moors.

It's about all the literary models Cervantes drew on: those ubiquitous romances of knight-errantry, but also Ovid's *Metamorphoses*, the Arcadian pastoral and the Greek tales of suffering for love. It's about the new technology of printing, about the way books provoke a revolution in thought that replaces old oral forms, systems of education, even religions, about our nostalgia for the old ways and the lore we have forgotten. It's about desire, absence and the pathos of logos. It's about the advent of modernity, the decline of courtliness and the rise of a class more concerned with gain than grace. Or it's about a man having a mid-life crisis and, instead of buying a red Mustang convertible or a Miata, he gets on his old horse and goes adventuring (this is the kind of stereotyped, common sense explanation Sancho would give if he were alive today—Sancho would be in sales, Teresa would be into Pilates and low-fat foods, and Sanchica would be at the nearest community college campus studying hotel management while working part-time at Wal-Mart).

Finally, it's about its own form, the structures, rhythms and repetitions, which enclose and organize all these characters, themes, and motifs. And when we have described these structures and their reflective or resonating functions, it becomes less clear how we can single out one theme as paramount. Form ensures that there will always be a surplus of meaning, something extra, a residue, so to speak, which contaminates our analytical certainty. This surplus is, perhaps among other things, the distance between the word and the thing the word represents, the distance between Alonso Quixano, Alonso the Good, and the woman he loves, a distance he can only attempt to cover on an old horse named Rozinante. Which is to say that if we look at the form itself it seems as if the novel incarnates the troubled passage from lover to loved one and from self to knowledge of what is really real. The story of one is the story of the other. Or, the novel—tale of suffering for love—mimes the machinery of cognition, the complex apparatus of desire, perception, imagination, repetition and memory by which we try to discern the shape of things. As Anne Carson writes,

> The same subterfuge which we have called an "erotic ruse" in novels and poems now appears to constitute the very structure of human thinking. When the mind reaches out to know, the space of desire opens and a necessary fiction transpires. (*Eros the Bittersweet*, 171)

Looking at form, when the tactical details are allowed to sink into the background, we see a pattern of desire, resistance and repetition (repetition of the main desire and resistance pattern and parallel—subplot—desire and resistance patterns). Desire precedes character, and what goes for character in a novel is really the particular acts and metonymic choices a character makes in the course of the story. Alonso Quixano, Alonso the Good, is a non-character.

No-one would want to read a book about him. It's only when Alonso, stricken with a sudden excess of desire and, identifying with his chivalric fantasies, transforms himself into Don Quixote that he comes to life as a character. The paradox (reading a book we are in a universe of multiplying paradoxes) is that Quixote seems most alive when he is most deluded, that is, when his actions suddenly become dramatically perverse, when his symptoms erupt.

Quixote's friends, the curate and the barber, and later student Carrasco, as well as the Duke and Duchess and all the other "readers" in the novel are similarly delighted with the new Don Quixote. They are entranced, suddenly taken out of themselves, as it were, as we ourselves as readers *of* the novel are. Their ambivalence about effecting a cure for the old don is one of the most interesting elements, an oscillation or flickering (that word again) that parallels the novel's own attitude to those chivalric romances. Ostensibly the novel is meant as a panegyric against knightly romances, but its delight in those popular stories is only too evident.

Rather than simply stick Quixote in a locked room, the curate and his friends assume a more creative and sympathetic stance toward his lunacy. The method they choose for curing him is to encourage and participate in his fantasy rather than deny it outright.

> And here the historian informs his readers, that when Sampson Carrasco advised Don Quixote to resume the profession of knight-errantry, it was in consequence of mature consultation between him, the curate, and the barber, when they deliberated upon the means of keeping him in peace and quiet at home, so that his brains, for the future, should not be disturbed in pursuit of those wild extravagancies; the result of which was, that the only way to cure the frenzy of this unhappy man, was at present not to check his ungovernable obstinacy, but, to humour it, and encourage him to go out again.... (2,15)

In Volume 1, chasing Quixote around La Mancha becomes the curate's quest, allowing him to dress up in costumes (the barber cross-dresses), travel and meet all sorts of interesting people. In the second volume, Carrasco, after egging Quixote on, turns knight-errant himself. As his squire, Thomas Cecial, says, he "is turned mad, that another knight may turn wise...." (2,8) When he finally defeats Quixote on that ill-famed beach in Barcelona, he doesn't demand that he renounce knight-errantry for good; instead, he merely sends Quixote home for a period of two years. And when Alonso the Good is dying in his bed, it is Carrasco who tries to breathe life into the old Christian by bringing him news that Dulcinea has been dis-enchanted.

This is a strange sort of psychotherapy, though perhaps no stranger than a lot of contemporary cures, from primal screams to orgone therapy and Iron Man group drumming scenes. It rather comically foreshadows Lacan's notion of traversing the fantasy as described by Slavoj Zizek in *Welcome to the Desert of the Real*. The conventional way of thinking of a psychotherapeutic cure involves encouraging the patient to abandon fantasy and face reality. Lacan turns this conventional cure upside down. Conventional reality (Sancho's reality) is a communally programmed virtual reality beyond which lurks a real Real (capital R) which cannot be directly accessed (this is something like Kant's distinction between the world of appearances and the noumenal world of things in themselves or Plato's distinction between the world of appearances and transcendental Ideas or Forms which underlie them; as I say, Lacan cannot escape the taint of dualism). Psychiatric symptoms, neuroses, fantasies are eruptions of this underlying reality into our experience of conventional reality. There is no bedrock reality as such; we experience either conventional reality (one sort of fiction) or a fantasy symptom (also a fiction) which, Janus-like, has some basis in the Real. As Zizek writes,

> The Real which returns has the status of a(nother) semblance: *precisely because it is real, that is, on account of its traumatic/excessive character, we are unable to integrate it into (what we experience as) our reality; and are therefore compelled to experience it as a nightmarish apparition*...the Real itself, in order to be sustained, has to be perceived as a nightmarish unreal spectre. (*Welcome to the Desert of the Real*, 19)

That is, the conventional world of reality (windmills) is to an extent an organized fiction (the world of appearances) and the only way we can experience the Real (nothingness, death, abyss, etc.) is to experience it as another fiction (fantasy, symptom).

Alice Munro expresses this beautifully in her story "Meneseteung" when the (eccentric and quixotic) spinster poetess Almeda Roth gets stoned and hallucinates on nerve medicine after rejecting the boorish advances of her neighbour, Jarvis Poulter.

> No need for alarm.
> For she hasn't thought that crocheted roses could float away or that tombstones could hurry down the street. She doesn't mistake that for reality, and neither does she mistake anything else for reality, and that is how she knows that she is sane.

This is in fact the kind of *uber*-sanity even Quixote shows from time to time, especially earlier in the novel when the memory of Aldonza Lorenzo is still fairly fresh in his mind.

> "...now, I remember, Dulcinea can neither read nor write, nor ever set eyes on any writing or letter of mine; for, our mutual love has been altogether platonic, without extending farther than a modest glance; and even that so seldom, that I can safely swear, in twelve years, during which I have loved her more than the light of these eyes, which will one day be closed in dust, I have not seen her more than four times, and even in these four times, perhaps, she has not perceived me looking at her more than once. Such is the restraint and reserve, in which her father Lorenzo Corchuelo, and her mother Aldonza Nogales, have brought her up! ...let it suffice, that I imagine and believe the worthy Aldonza Lorenzo, to be beautiful and modest...and these two is Dulcinea in consummate possession of.... And to conclude, I imagine that all I have said is true without exaggeration or diminution. I paint her in my fancy, according to my wish, as well in beauty as in rank...and let people say what they will, if I am blamed by the ignorant, I shall be acquitted by the most rigid of those who are proper judges of the case." (1,25)

That is, as he descends into the fantasy of knight-errantry, Quixote is sometimes aware that he is functioning in two separate reality discourses and simply choosing to act in one as opposed to the other without necessarily deciding which is more real.

Cervantes keeps comically flipping these discourses to the very end of the novel, which is in keeping with the nature of his book as a relativity machine. On his deathbed, Quixote avers that he has returned to sanity and renounces "all the profane histories of knight-errantry...which, I, from dear-bought experience, abominate and abhor." (2,74) But his friends, having traversed so much of the fantasy themselves, can no longer recognize the discourse of "sanity" or conventional reality when it speaks to them. Instead of rejoicing at his "cure" they attempt to cure him of his cure by reinstating the order of fantasy (comedy of reversal).

> The three friends, hearing this declaration, believed he was certainly seized with some new species of madness; and, on this supposition, Sampson replied, "Now, signor Don Quixote, when we have received the news of my lady Dulcinea's being disinchanted, do you talk at this rate? when we are on the point of becoming shepherds, that we may pass away our time happily in singing...no more of that, I beseech you: recollect your spirits, and leave off talking such idle stories." (2,74)

Quixote's return to "sanity" is so sudden and inexplicable that momentarily his friends see the discourse of social and religious orthodoxy for what it really is, another fiction, a "new species of madness," and an idle story. And they quite correctly interpret his discourse switch as the prelude to death. That is, as soon as he starts expressing himself in sentiments "so rational, so christian and well-connected" (2,74), they realize the end is near. And the end, of course, is the ultimate and final eruption of the Real, as it were, which, as Sancho assures Quixote, is better faced as a story than with melancholy acceptance (or as Zizek writes, "deprived of its fantasmatic support" (*Welcome to the Desert of the Real*, 21)).

> "Lack-a-day! dear sir, cried Sancho, blubbering, do not die —take my advice, and live many years upon the face of the earth; for, the greatest madness a man can be guilty of in this life, is to let himself die outright, without being slain by any person whatever, or destroyed by any other weapon than the hands of melancholy. Heark ye, signor, hang sloth; get up and let us take the field.... (2,74)

Which is to say, as I have said before, that *Don Quixote* is not a novel about fantasy and reality with Sancho representing the latter. It deploys a much more nimble, subtle and complex argument than that. On the level of form, it recognizes that a book is a book, and character is symptom. On the level of language, it recognizes the fictional (narrative) nature of reality. On the level of psychology, it recognizes the functional role of fantasy, the eruption of symptom as a displacement of the Real. In effect, Quixote's fantasy is what he is and his embracing the fantasy is, to his friends and readers alike, a source of surprise and delight. And this is not to mention the Duke and Duchess who take a tremendous pleasure in treating him like a knight-errant and concocting hoaxes that function within the libidinal economy of his imaginative universe.

The sentimental dream-the-impossible-dream school of Quixote criticism reads this delight as evidence of our admiration for people who stand up for their beliefs, dreams and ideals. But that's not really what appears to be going on. Quixote's friends don't admire him for his ideals, for his chaste love for Dulcinea, for the poetry in his soul. They like him because he is surprising and entertaining, because he says wise things while also violently spreading chaos wherever he goes, interrupting the placid and boring day-to-dayness of things. As Zizek suggests, this banal day-to-dayness is itself "a defence-formation against the threat embodied in the fantasy." (*Welcome to the Desert of the Real*, 21) Quixote's identification with his knightly love fantasy seems, paradoxically, to allow him to become himself which is, in the end, a perverse symptom, an acting out. It's oddly liberating, and its effect is to liberate others. The dark side of acting out is the loneliness and anxiety he clearly feels when, from time to time, the fantasy begins to fade. His insomnia, his violent rages when mocked, and his paralytic fear of seduction all bespeak a troubled conscience and a fear that the world will turn out to be less exciting than he thinks it is.

Like Sancho, the curate, Carrasco, the Duke and the Duchess, we love characters in books precisely because of their commitment to their fantasies, the metonymic objects of their desire and the perverse contortions (dramas) they enact to try to acquire them. Such a commitment is not just romantic; it's transgressive in relation to the fiction of normality. It means somehow turning things inside out, actually living the fantasy, which normally we use to deflect or repress the tumult of inchoate desire and anxiety inside us. We live in a tightly lidded world, a narrowly defined band of so-called reality (the doughnut ring of social, linguistic and cultural licence) between the inner (self) and outer silence. There is a breathtaking and deeply attractive (if not socially admirable) honesty in the way Quixote allows himself to go crazy, to inhabit his fantasy. And, of course, what he inhabits is a strange world of necromancers, chaste ladies, castles, knights, giants and images of death. In other words, he reinvents himself in the stuff of nightmarish dreams where what seems real can transmogrify in a flash into something horrifyingly dangerous or seductive. A symptom is thus an eruption of the real into the so-called real. In truth, the symptom isn't any more real than anything else. But we, as readers, are always gleeful when we see one because it is a message, if coded and garbled, from beyond, a sign of life.

We live in a strange world. Language has emptied the self of being. We fill this self-void with symptoms. What we know of ourselves comes from understanding symptoms. My marriage has broken down, I'm an alcoholic, I lost my job and I'm depressed, therefore I am. On one level, what Quixote is after is what we are all after. Call it a moment of true feeling (after a Peter Handke title) or love or authenticity (after the existentialists) or grace or flow or transcendence or *unio mystico* or wisdom or simply knowledge. He suffers from a passion for the Real, to use a phrase Zizek borrows from Alain Badiou (*Welcome to the Desert of the Real*, 6). And as it happens, the road to the Real (again, that Lacanian Real with the upper case R) is not the common sense road of 'growing up' or 'getting real.' In fact the common sense world, the utterly banal universe of Sancho's folksy adages, though comic and familiar, is the opposite of reality. It's the world of the normal, the habitual and the stereotyped, the world of the recognizably real as opposed to a reality that we might not recognize, that might hit us with the force of an hallucination or a mystical experience or a nervous breakdown.

But our passion for the real is thus paradoxical. We want it and we probably don't want it at the same time. In *Don Quixote*, there is a real woman named Aldonza Lorenzo, an illiterate, buxom, healthy, brawny peasant girl. Alonso the Good has been admiring her from a distance (and mostly in his fancy) for twelve years. Alonso Quixano's passion for the real leads to his perverse re-invention of himself as a knight-errant and Aldonza as the chaste and beautiful Dulcinea who doesn't exist. In effect, his passion for the real actually becomes an excuse not to grapple with a real woman.

For twelve years, Alonso has been suppressing his desire for Aldonza. His failure to act is no doubt due to class and social differences. When, as Don Quixote, he approaches a peasant woman on a donkey outside Toboso near the beginning of Volume 2, he is appalled at her gross physicality which he excoriates in class terms.

> "...robbing her [Dulcinea], at the same time, of that which is so peculiar to ladies of fashion, I mean that sweet scent which is the result of their living among flowers and perfume; for, know, my friend, when I went to lift Dulcinea upon her palfrey, as thou sayest it was, tho' to me, it seemed neither more nor less than a she-ass, I was almost suffocated and poisoned with a whiff of undigested garlic!" (2,10)

When he finally decides to act on his desire he goes in precisely the wrong direction. He creates a metonymic or fetishized fantasy; he exhibits a symptom; he goes mad (which may tell us more about the way men interact with women than we care to face). His love gets in the way of love.

Thus Cervantes invents that peculiarly modern version of the passion for the real which is itself a fantasy of a reality. This point is driven home late in the novel when Quixote encounters that delightful little group of idle young people masquerading as shepherds and shepherdesses. Nowadays, one thinks of all those trendy and commercially available avenues to authenticity from cheap air fares to Bali to organic foods, reality TV, amateur porn, and clothes that look like they are worn by poor people. One of the things that makes *Don Quixote* a great novel is the way Cervantes insists on ironizing and subverting the old knight's dream of the real thing. Quixote's object of desire is neither plausible nor achievable. But we love Quixote for this because, in his madness, he displays a certain relative honesty; his behaviour is at least a confession that the reality erupting beneath the apparently tranquil exterior of his life (those twelve years of inaction) is too much for him to bear. We would love to blurt out our own anxiety, throw off inhibition and prudence, give in to desire and fantasy. As readers, we dip our toes chastely into the millrace of desire; we fantasize giving into fantasy, much as the curate and Carrasco do in the novel.

The Thematic Matrix of the Novel

At the beginning of the modern era, a failed tax collector named Cervantes took some old forms, near at hand—the Greek novel, the chivalric romance, the Arcadian pastoral—and reforged them in light of his insights into the effects of the new technologies of writing and books. *Don Quixote* is a stunningly complex arrangement of new and old themes which is as contemporary now as it was then because our circumstances have only changed in degree not in their essential structure. The invention of computer and communications technologies has only extended the networking and storage capacity of the book. The book gave birth to the individual then eviscerated it of content. The Romantic Movement was a bourgeois spasm of quixotic symptom formation, an unconscious protest against the fading of the self. Like Quixote, we are haunted by the real, lurch about attaching ourselves to this or that version, always dubious of our own allegiances.

Don Quixote's miraculous modernity stems from two factors: 1) its bookishness and its general recognition of relativity and the linguistic nature of self and reality; and 2) its recognition of our heart-sinking, sentimental attachment to particular versions of reality (love). Cervantes was neither a metaphysician nor a proto-analyst; he chose to write a novel, not to prove a point but rather to try something in the nature of a variation on a set of themes and to tell us how it feels to be a human. Everything he says is paradoxical along the lines of the dilemma of the Cretan barber who said, All Cretans are liars. All the novel's claims for truth are fictional; hence, again, *Don Quixote*'s flickering quality, the alternating-current ironies that reflect the Janus-like or di-polar nature of existence (experience, thought).

This flickering quality, which says as much about our sentimental human attachment to moments of being and illusions of self as it does about the nature of consciousness and reality, the mysterious complexity of being, can yet create moments of tearing sadness, of loss and yearning. When Quixote kneels before the horse trough during the night of his vigil, when he tries to ride Rozinante toward the thudding hammers of the fulling mill, when he discourses to Sancho and the mule drivers about the portraits of the warrior saints, and when he weeps over his torn stocking at the Duke's castle, he becomes more than a madman or a figure of fun. With a novel, the mistake is always to try to fix such moments, to say this or that event defines the whole (those windmills, for example, have gotten fixed in the public mind). Cervantes does everything he can to keep the accent of meaning moving from sentence to sentence. The novel flickers from grand emotion to pratfall to slapstick violence.

The truth is Lionel Trilling was half right when he said "all prose fiction is a variation on the theme of *Don Quixote*." First of all, *Don Quixote* isn't about a single theme (say, appearance and reality, as Trilling suggested). This is the reductive either-or mentality Kundera castigates in his essay on the don in *The Art of the Novel*.

> What does Cervantes' great novel mean? Much has been written on the question. Some see in it a rationalist critique of Don Quixote's hazy idealism. Others see it as a celebration of that same idealism. Both interpretations are mistaken because they both seek at the novel's core not on inquiry but a moral position.... This "either-or" encapsulates an inability to tolerate the essential relativity of things human, an inability to look squarely at the absence of the Supreme Judge. This inability makes the novel's wisdom (the wisdom of uncertainty) hard to accept and understand. (*The Art of the Novel*, 7)

Instead *Don Quixote* seems to deploy a cluster or basket of themes which animate, reflect and modify one another: love, desire, books, reading, versions of reality, identity, insanity, language, genre, form, class and marriage, to name a few. Cervantes marches under the banner of complexity; every sentence reminds us that the situation is not as simple as we thought it was.

This thematic cluster forms a coherent network or system which we can see threading its way through the history of Euro-Western literature. It is truly quixotic as opposed to the eccentric idealism we commonly associate with the word. It is also truly novelistic, that is, it defines the totality of thematic and formal possibilities open to the novel and forges them into a single work. Though some critics have been loath to call it a novel at all, *Don Quixote* is actually the type, the template, of all novels.

All novels are more or less quixotic in this sense, though certain things critics and even novelists say about novels can confuse the issue. Confusion centres around the troublesome word "realism." The quixotic thematic bundle is not exactly modern, if we associate modernity itself with ideas of reason, progress, the individual, liberal economics, the rise of nation-states, etc. Modernity is an interim cultural construct that replaces theology with a belief in the self and facts. Its novel aesthetic favours verisimilitude (what Northrop Frye called the low mimetic) whereas *Don Quixote*'s aesthetic only includes verisimilitude as one of a number of possible narrative options (*sometimes* Don Quixote seems very real). But even the most realistic novels are only successful insofar as they create a fictional world of metonymic desire, obsessive plot repetitions and battling discourses (call them different characters or points of view). There are two kinds of novelist: the one who plays the verisimilitude card to the hilt and tells us the book he is writing is a mirror of the real world and the one who admits that the real world is just another book. But they are both writing fiction.

The thematic matrix of the novel underlies or inheres in form itself; that is, form and content coincide, or form creates content. Kundera overstates his case when he says that the history of the European novel has depreciated the legacy of *Don Quixote* by too slavish adherence to "the imperative of verisimilitude." Verisimilitude is a technique that only becomes problematic when someone tries to turn it into a definition. (And to be sure this happens fairly often with unthinking writers and journalist-critics.) As André Brink writes in his introduction to *The Novel, Language and Narrative from Cervantes to Calvino*,

> ...Realism itself opened up whole new landscapes to be explored by the novel in its inherence in language. Joyce is

not only the heir of Sterne but also of Defoe and Fielding. Inasmuch as Realism came to be perceived as the 'only' Great Tradition of the novel, of course it has a pernicious influence. But it seems unfair to blame the *novel* for the restricted vision of a *critical* tradition endorsed by Ian Watt. (*The Novel*, 6)

The truth is the cluster of themes that define the totality of novel discourse, the thematic matrix constructed by Cervantes, has persisted through the history of the novel. I don't mean just the obvious imitators of *Don Quixote*, though there are plenty of those. I mean that the thematic matrix stands behind every novel. Sometimes it is submerged, almost hidden behind a camouflage of verisimilitude (the text exerting itself to deny that it's a text). And there are certainly a lot of bad or second-rate novels which, either through faulty construction or didacticism, deny the matrix. Didacticism is an especially interesting departure from the novel model; the thematic matrix is against totalizing messages of any kind. In a true novel, any totalizing message is ripe for ironic deflation or it gets in a fight with another totalizing message.

What I find particularly fascinating and delightful are the works in which the quixotic theme bundle rises to the surface of a text, intact, as it were, without the author making an explicit connection with the *Don Quixote* model. This is a bit like butterfly collecting. Examples pop up here and there, more often than one would expect and often in surprising places, works more or less known for their authenticity or realism. In such instances, the Cervantean thematic cluster seems to emerge out of an intelligent author's dialogue with the form itself.

In Jane Austen's *Mansfield Park*, for example, Fanny Price, the protagonist, is a reader (which makes her suspicious in the eyes of the ineffable Aunt Norris) and a book collector, and, like Quixote, she's in love with someone but can't act on her love. This time the social class problem is inverted; Fanny is too far beneath Edmund Bertram to hope to marry him. In other words, we might think of *Mansfield Park* as *Don Quixote* written from the point of view of Aldonza Lorenzo.

The English upper class tribal rules of courtesy, interest and capital preservation guarantee the Bertram family a life of genteel superficiality, which just barely conceals the dark reality of racism, slavery, and British imperial hegemony. When Sir Thomas Bertram, the father, leaves home to fix affairs in his plantations, the house rules suddenly relax and the children give in to their libidinal fantasies. Among other things, they put on a play in the billiard-room with hilarious consequences that echo the multiple arguments against chivalric romances or the bearded duenna's rant against poetry in *Don Quixote*. Before rehearsals, Fanny's mind is a tumult of Platonic apprehension.

> The whole subject of it was love—a marriage of love was to be described by the gentleman, and very little short of a declaration of love made by the lady.
>
> She had read, and read the scene again with many painful, many wondering emotions, and looked forward to their representation of it as a circumstance almost too interesting. (*Mansfield Park*, 139)

Once again books are to blame for leading people astray and encouraging them to find inappropriate love partners. But in *Mansfield Park* Sir Thomas returns and ultimately restores order and the rule of law (there is even a book-burning). And Fanny Price gets to marry Edmund even though he has made a fool of himself over the delightful, if morally flawed, Mary Crawford, his Dulcinea. As in *Don Quixote*, the delightful people, the ones who seem a have a bit of energy and life, are flawed and socially disruptive—especially Mary and her handsome brother Henry (who function something like the Duke and Duchess in *Don Quixote*) —whereas the good people, Edmund and Fanny, are restrained, careful and a bit dull. Austen gives Henry Crawford the last word on the pleasures of libidinal explosions, play-acting and fantasy formation in a speech that somehow resonates with what we as readers feel like at the end of a novel or what Carrasco and Sancho seem to feel as they try to reignite Quixote's chivalric mania.

> "It is as a dream, a pleasant dream?" he exclaimed, break-ing forth again after a few minutes of musing. "I shall always look back on our theatrical with exquisite pleasure. There was such an interest, such an animation, such a spirit diffused! Everybody felt it. We were all alive. There was

employment, hope, solicitude, bustle, for every hour of the day. Always some little objection, some little doubt, some little anxiety to be gotten over. I was never happier." (*Mansfield Park*, 187)

After all that's happened in the course of the novel, the marriage of Edmund and Fanny seems oddly forced, as if Jane Austen intended to emphasize the rule of social restraint to the detriment of whatever personal karma her characters might have accrued through their suffering. Fanny deserves better than Edmund. Frye seems to notice this when he writes:

> In Jane Austen's other novels the realistic study of character and setting is related, somewhat quizzically, to a romantic story with a conventionally happy ending.... ("The Renaissance of Books")

But as in most instances of this kind, the romantic story, the happy ending, the marriage at the close, conduce to confirm the reintroduction of social codes, not to mention common sense, respect for private property, and conventional reality. The sacrament of marriage serves to erase any evidence of the tear in the fabric of normality created by the eruption of libidinal energy or the reality that isn't recognized as such, that is, the Real. Marriage (the sacramental form of true love) tends always to be a marker for normalcy and social orthodoxy. If we compare *Mansfield Park* with a novel that is actually quite similar in many ways, John Fowles' *The French Lieutenant's Woman*, we see an author again baring the device of the comforting lie by offering not just one but two possible endings, the romantic marriage ending and the ending in which the woman becomes an independent operator while the quixotic hero lives alone.

In Alice Munro's short story "Meneseteung," the nineteenth-century spinster poetess Almeda Roth (reader and minor author) takes the role of Quixote. The story is told from an outsider position, by an authorial first-person narrator, much the same as in *Don Quixote*, who reconstructs events based on gravestone inscriptions, old poetry collections and newspaper clippings. The townspeople and their little newspaper, the *Vidette*, function, like the curate, the barber, the canon of Toledo, and all the other nominally "sane" observers in *Don Quixote*, as the voice of social authority and conventional opinion. And once again, much as in the novel, the crux of Almeda's oddity turns on her relation to love and books. Marriage is the socially acceptable and utilitarian erotic outcome; reading books gets in the way. Note how, like Quixote, Almeda is "gloomy" and "all that reading and poetry—it seemed more of a drawback, a barrier, an obsession...." (Also, like Quixote, she suffers from insomnia.)

Almeda's Aldonza Lorenzo is the businessman Jarvis Poulter who deals in salt mines. Almeda wants to marry and even has a sex fantasy which, comically enough, involves Jarvis coming to bed in his longjohns with his hat on. Their courtship evolves as a non-dialogue between two different discourses or descriptions of reality. Poulter's landscape is industrial, pragmatic and realistic, while Almeda will always be imagining the sweep of history, changes in environment, and the romance of Indians and early explorers. When they are together, she is "sorry to have the countryside removed for her—filmed over, in a way, by his talk and preoccupations."

Unlike Quixote, who eventually renounces his fantasy (and, one supposes, Aldonza herself), Almeda chooses to live under the sign of dream, breaks off her relationship with Poulter, remains unmarried, takes nerve medicine, and keeps writing her poems. She remains quixotic until her death many years later, and her obituary, published in the *Vidette*, echoes the madness of the old don himself.

> It is a sad misfortune that in later years the mind of this fine person had become somewhat clouded and her behaviour, in consequence, somewhat rash and unusual. Her attention to decorum and to the care and adornment of her person had suffered, to the degree that she had become, in the eyes of those unmindful of her former pride and daintiness, a familiar eccentric, or even, sadly, a figure of fun.

This is not to say, of course, that Alice Munro or Jane Austen were using *Don Quixote* as a model. But these three works of fiction, as I've suggested, share a thematic matrix expressed in character types, relations and plot motifs, which persist in the cultural sentence of modernity. They also demonstrate a range of possible outcomes, as if authors were running a series of experiments on the nature of the human and the real. In *Don Quixote*, for no particular plot reason, Quixote simply renounces his madness (and books of chivalry) and dies. In *Mansfield Park*, Aldonza (Fanny) and Quixote (Edmund Bertram) get married. In both, the fiction of social consensus papers over a rift left by the eruption of libido and fantasy. In *Don Quixote*, Quixote himself fixes things by reverting to the discourse of orthodoxy; in *Mansfield Park*, the author forces the acceptable outcome onto her characters. In "Meneseteung," there is no marriage and no renunciation, but the point of view moves to the town newspaper, which effectively quarantines and disarms Almeda's peculiarities by labelling them clouded, rash and unusual. In both *Don Quixote* and "Meneseteung," narrative irony imposes a different reading wherein social orthodoxy and the conventions of realism are called into question. And, as I have mentioned, Alice Munro's story contains an explicit statement of the fictional nature of all realities and their relation to the notion of sanity. Jane Austen, on the other hand, uses a moral cudgel to let us know that, despite her earlier ironies, the marriage of Edmund and Fanny is a good thing.

Finally (I am rigorously disciplining myself to give only three examples), if *Mansfield Park* is a version of *Don Quixote* written from Aldonza Lorenzo's point of view, then Joseph Conrad's "Heart of Darkness" is the same story written from the point of view of Sampson Carrasco. Conrad's protagonist, Marlow, sent to Africa to pilot a riverboat in the interior, finds himself caught up in an expedition to retrieve the madman Kurtz (a painter and a writer). Kurtz, like Quixote, has a real woman in his life, the woman the story calls his Intended. But their relationship seems distant and restrained in all senses. We don't know how long Kurtz has intended to marry his Intended, but he has been in Africa a long time, and we catch fleeting glimpses of that other, nearly mythic African woman, the heart of darkness herself, his Dulcinea, who has replaced his Intended in his fantasy.

In a sense Kurtz is Quixote and Sancho combined since, like Sancho, his ambition isn't simply for love (that seems rather incidental to the plot) but for power. The fantasy he traverses is an extension of the capitalist-colonial dream with the brakes of prudence and common sense removed. In this light, Sancho's little fantasy about gaining a governorship in Africa and selling his subjects as slaves seems presciently Kurtzian. Like Quixote, Kurtz exhibits a strange mixture of lucidity and delusion.

> And I wasn't arguing with a lunatic either. Believe me or not, his intelligence was perfectly clear.... But his soul was mad.... Sometimes he was contemptibly childish. He desired to have kings meet him at railway stations on his return from some ghastly Nowhere, where he intended to accomplish great things.

Likewise Marlow isn't simply Sampson Carrasco on a quest to bring back Quixote; more precisely he's a combination of the student-knight and Cid Hamet Benengeli. Conrad's text insistently reminds us of the narrative machinery, the smoke and mirrors, of Cervantes. The story is actually told by an unnamed first-person authorial narrator, a passenger on a boat moored in the Thames. Marlow tells his story to the narrator and the other passengers, old friends, and fills it with reflective surfaces, analogies, and doubts.

> "...No, it is impossible; it is impossible to convey the life-sensation of any given epoch of one's existence—that which makes its truth, its meaning—its subtle and pene-trating essence. It is impossible. We live, as we dream—alone."
> He paused again as if reflecting, then added—"Of course in this you fellows see more than I could then. You see me, who you know...."
> It had become so pitch dark that we listeners could hardly see one another....

Kurtz dies before he can return to so-called civilization, and Marlow who has tracked him into the heart of darkness nearly succumbs as well. But one of the most curious things about the story is the way it ends with Marlow's odd, anticlimactic visit to Kurtz's Intended. He finds he cannot tell Kurtz's fiancé the truth about her lover's last words because it "would have been too dark—too dark altogether...." (The inconclusive ellipsis is Conrad's.) Instead he tells her Kurtz died with her name on his lips. Marlow's comforting lie is the hinge or keystone of an unreal version of real-ity. He tells the lie in order to preserve the Intended's illusion of true love, marriage and conventional reality. But in telling the lie,

Marlow makes explicit the fictional nature of reality to his listeners (and his readers).

What's fascinating about Marlow's lie is that, to use Shklovsky's phrase, Conrad bares the device of fictional consensus. Marlow hates to lie because, as he says, a lie smells of death. At the end of *Don Quixote*, there is a lie as well. Sampson Carrasco tells the ailing knight "we have received news of Dulcinea's being disen- chanted." Carrasco worries that Quixote is dying, and he concludes that reanimating his love interest will help him live. In essence, they are the same lie (something about true love). Both lies attest to the human need to rely on some version of reality, in Zizek's phrase some form of fantasmatic support; both lies confess the fictive nature of beliefs we hold most dear. This is where the paradox of the novel winds itself into a spiral of immense density, almost opaque. The truth is "too dark" for Kurtz's Intended. Sancho begs Quixote to "take the field in shepherd's apparel" again and not to let himself be destroyed by melancholy.

Under the sign of life, the fiction becomes a necessary truth.

The End

All great novels seem to strain against their own complex truths, truths that can only be uttered as paradoxes or nearly incoherent outbursts or assuaged with comforting lies. If novels enact symptoms, endings are often about damage control if only because the truth is "too dark." This truth is what Kundera calls the wisdom of uncertainty.

> To take, with Cervantes, the world as ambiguity, to be obliged to face not a single absolute truth but a welter of contradictory truths (truths embodied in *imaginary selves* called characters), to have as one's only certainty the *wisdom of uncertainty*.... (*The Art of the Novel*, 6-7)

But form itself can be a kind of comforting lie, forcing order on what is essentially chaotic. This is why the greatest books must always be against books, must strive to become something other than a book—a prophecy, a chant, a prayer, a keen, a cry. They address the unspeakable essence of things by exposing the beautiful, complex relativity machine of our fictive reality.

At the end of *Don Quixote* the old knight recovers his sanity, renounces knight-errantry and books of chivalry, and dies, but his death is anticlimactic, his sanity a bit bewildering to his readers (both inside and outside the novel). In a sense, he is already dead, passing away for the first time on the beach at Barcelona, when, at the novel's plot climax, calamitously defeated by the Knight of the White Moon, Quixote resigns himself to death in the name of his lady Dulcinea.

The scene is shockingly abrupt, dreamlike and uncanny as befits an eruption of the Real. The old knight's final defeat, after all his adventures, comes with astonishing swiftness. When Carrasco appears on the beach, carrying a shield with a white moon painted on it, he intones:

> "I the knight of the white moon, whose unheard-of exploits, may, peradventure, recal him to your remembrance, am come with hostile intent to prove the force of thine arm; to convince and compel thee to own that my mistress,

whosoever she is, exceeds in beauty thy Dulcinea del Toboso...." (2, 64)

He is a mysterious lunar knight, champion of the unnameable
female, hero from beyond the reach of words. Capturing the spirit if
not the letter, Smollett calls him "this romantic stranger," though I
consulted three other translations in which the word "romantic"
does not appear. Sancho watches Quixote thrown down and crushed,
but to him "it seemed to be a dream." When Quixote speaks, it is
with a "languid tone, and feeble voice, that seemed to issue from a
tomb." When help arrives, his rescuers find him "pale as death, and
his forehead bedewed with cold sweat."

Defeated with a finality (not to mention inevitability) that even
he cannot ignore or explain away (those enchanters), Quixote offers
his life rather than admit Dulcinea isn't as beautiful as what's-her-
name. This is an apocalyptic moment. After an instant of reflection,
the astonished Quixote realizes that his fantasy, his symptom, is
more substantial than he is, that the fictive real in which he has
been operating can go on perfectly well without him. His only
option, then, is to sacrifice himself rather than discredit Dulcinea by
his inability to live up to his dream. In his tomb-voice, he tells the
White Moon Knight:

> "Dulcinea del Toboso is the most beautiful woman in the
> world, and I the most unfortunate knight on earth; and, as
> it is not reasonable that my weakness should discredit this
> truth, make use of your weapon, knight, and instantly
> deprive me of life...." (2,64)

But the Knight of the White Moon turns away, only binding
him to leave the practice of knight-errantry for two years and go
home. By imitation, Quixote has tried to reinvent himself as both a
Grail knight and the wounded king of legend; when he tries to
sacrifice himself, the Knight of the White Moon refuses the gesture,
much as the Lord of the Israelites refused Abraham's sacrifice of
Isaac. History, modernity and the novel begin when the gods refuse
our ancient sacrifices and condemn us to absence.

The end of a novel is like a death, a simulacrum of death, which
is to say that at the end of *Don Quixote* the death room is crowded
with readers all wishing, like Carrasco and Sancho, to revive the

knight's desire. Symptom, book, self and life are somehow coterminous, and the melancholy apathy into which Quixote has fallen, according to Sancho's diagnosis of the situation, is the opposite of all four, a living death, a prelude to the grave. "Heark ye, signor," Sancho says,

> hang sloth; get up and let us take the field in shepherd's apparel, according to our agreement: who knows, but behind some bush we may find my lady Dulcinea disinchanted, and a comely sight for to see." (2,74)

Sancho, so apt in the discourse of his master's madness, briefly turns writer and, composing the bridge to a new book, starts feeding him lines, suggesting evasive rationales for his defeat in Barcelona in the old vein, even citing, finally, those very books of chivalry which were the cause of all the trouble.

> "If you take your overthrow so much to heart, lay the blame at my door, and say you was vanquished by my carelessness, in girting Rozinante; besides, your worship must have read in your books of chivalry, that it was common for one knight to unhorse another, and for him who was vanquished to-day, to be victor to-morrow." (2,74)

Which is to say that, at the end, the squire has understood the lesson of the novel: in our fictional universe, books teach us to be real.

A Note on the Translation

I read Tobias Smollett's translation which was published in 1755 and reprinted in 1986 with an introduction by Carlos Fuentes. The edition I have makes citing chapters difficult. Smollett used a volume, book and chapter setup no other translation I glanced at uses. And he (or his printer) managed to omit the chapter division between Chapter 13 and Chapter 14 of Volume 1, and, in Volume 2, Chapter 68 and Chapter 69 are given the same number. This meant I had to renumber the chapters by hand in my copy so that my references would agree with every other modern version of *Don Quixote*. Also Smollett used commas and quotation marks in a manner less precise than we are accustomed to today. I found this eccentricity endearingly quixotic and did not try to correct him.

Fortunately and somewhat miraculously, Barnes & Noble Classics has just (2004) reprinted a cheap edition of Smollett's translation revised by Carole Slade (with the lovely Gustave Doré illustrations sprinkled throughout). Smollett called the two parts of *Don Quixote* Volume 1 and Volume 2 (a practice I followed); Slade has altered this usage to the more generally accepted designations Part 1 and Part 2. She also renumbered the chapters correctly and modernized some of Smollett's spelling (thus Rozinante becomes Rocinante)—though, thankfully, she preserved the eccentric punctuation. All of which makes this new edition an excellent and accessible companion to *The Enamoured Knight*.

I also consulted translations by Burton Raffel, Walter Starkie and John Ormsby as well as the new translation by Edith Grossman. I found them all helpful here and there, especially Ormsby. But I had grown fond of Smollett's zest, his linguistic élan. Reading more up-to-date translations was a bit like reading a contemporary Good News version of the Bible after growing up with the King James.

Auerbach, E. *Mimesis*. Princeton, 1968.

Austen, J. *Mansfield Park*. Edited with an Introduction and Notes by Kathryn Sutherland. London, 1996.

Bakhtin, M. *The Dialogic Imagination*. Translated by Caryl Emerson and Michael Holquist. Austin, 1981.

—————. *Rabelais and His World*. Translated by Hélène Iswolsky. Bloomington, 1984.

Barzun, J. *From Dawn to Decadence, 1500 to the Present, 500 Years of Western Cultural Life*. New York, 2000.

Benjamin, W. *Illuminations*. Translated by Harry Zohn. New York, 1968.

Bloom, H., Ed. *Miguel de Cervantes*. New York, 1987.

Borges, J. *Labyrinths*. New York, 1970.

Brink, A. *The Novel, Language and Narrative from Cervantes to Calvino*. New York, 1998.

Brown, E. *Rhythm in the Novel*. Toronto, 1950.

Carson, A. *Eros the Bittersweet*. Normal, 1998.

Cervantes. *Don Quixote de le Mancha*. Translated by Tobias Smollett. New York, 1986.

—————. *Don Quixote*. Translated by Tobias Smollett. Revised by Carole Slade. New York, 2004.

—————. *Don Quixote*. Translated by Burton Raffel. New York, 1996.

—————. *Don Quixote of La Mancha*. Translated by Walter Starkie. London, 1957.

—————. *Don Quixote*. Translated by John Ormsby. London, 1922. Available as Project Gutenberg Etext, 1997.

Conrad, J. *Heart of Darkness and The Secret Sharer*. With an introduction, biographical sketch, and a selection of background materials and commentaries by Franklin Walker. New York, 1969.

Crump, M. *The Epyllion from Theocritus to Ovid*. Oxford, 1931.

De Madariaga, S. *Don Quixote, An Introductory Essay in Psychology*. Oxford, 1935.

De Rougement, D. *Love in the Western World*. Translated by Montgomery Belgion. New York, 1956.

Donald, M. *Origins of the Modern Mind, Three Stages in the Evolution of Culture and Cognition.* Cambridge, 1991.

Forster, E. *Aspects of the Novel.* London, 1927.

Foucault, M. *The Order of Things, An Archaeology of the Human Sciences.* New York, 1970.

Frappier-Mazur, L. *Writing the Orgy, Power and Parody in Sade.* Translated by Gillian C. Gill. Philadelphia, 1996.

Frye, N. *Anatomy of Criticism.* Princeton, 1971.

—————. *The Secular Scripture, A Study of the Structure of Romance.* Cambridge, 1976.

—————. "The Renaissance of Books". *Spiritus Mundi: Essays on Literature, Myth, and Society.* Bloomington, 1976.

Girard, R. *Deceit, Desire, and the Novel, The Self and Other in Literary Structure.* Translated by Yvonne Freccero. Baltimore, 1966.

—————. "From 'The Divine Comedy' to the Sociology of the Novel." *Sociology of Literature & Drama.* London, 1973.

Goody, J. *The Logic of Writing and the Organization of Society.* Cambridge, 1986.

Kermode, F. *The Sense of an Ending.* Oxford, 1966.

Kundera, M. *The Art of the Novel.* Translated by Linda Asher. New York, 1988.

Loomis, S. and Loomis, L., Ed. *Medieval Romances.* New York, 1957.

Lukens-Olson, C. "Heroics of Persuasion in *Los trabajos de Persiles y Sigismunda.*" *Cervantes: Bulletin of the Cervantes Society of America,* 21.2, 2001.

Martin, H-J. *The History and Power of Writing.* Translated by Lydia G. Cochrane. Chicago, 1994.

McLuhan, M. *The Gutenberg Galaxy, The Making of Typographic Man.* Toronto, 1962.

Munro, A. "Meneseteung" from *Friend of my Youth.* New York, 1990.

Nabokov, V. *Lectures on Don Quixote.* New York, 1983.

Ortega y Gasset, J. *Meditations on Quixote.* Translated by Evelyn Rugg and Diego Marin. New York, 1963.

Plato. *The Dialogues of Plato.* Translated by Benjamin Jowett. London, 1970.

Ross, W. *Aristotle Selections.* New York, 1938.

Shklovsky, V. *Theory of Prose.* Translated by Benjamin Sher. Normal, 1990.

Stevick, S., Ed. *The Theory of the Novel*. New York, 1967.

Todorov, T. *The Conquest of America, The Question of the Other*. Translated by Richard Howard. New York, 1984.

——————. *Mikhail Bakhtin, The Dialogical Principle*. Translated by Wlad Godzich. Minneapolis, 1984.

Watt, I. *The Rise of the Novel*. London, 1957.

Weston, J. *From Ritual to Romance*. New York, 1957.

Zizek, S. *Welcome to the Desert of the Real*. New York, 2002.

ABOUT THE AUTHOR

Douglas Glover is the author of four novels and four short story collections, including *Elle* (which won the Governor General's Award), *The Life and Times of Captain N.*, and *Bad News of the Heart*. He is also the author of a collection of essays, *Notes Home from a Prodigal Son*, and currently teaches at Vermont College.

SELECTED DALKEY ARCHIVE PAPERBACKS

FOR A FULL LIST OF PUBLICATIONS, VISIT:
www.dalkeyarchive.com

SELECTED DALKEY ARCHIVE PAPERBACKS

CAROLE MASO, *AVA.*
LADISLAV MATEJKA AND KRYSTYNA POMORSKA, EDS.,
  Readings in Russian Poetics: Formalist and
  Structuralist Views.
HARRY MATHEWS,
  The Case of the Persevering Maltese: Collected Essays.
  Cigarettes.
  The Conversions.
  The Human Country: New and Collected Stories.
  The Journalist.
  My Life in CIA.
  Singular Pleasures.
  The Sinking of the Odradek Stadium.
  Tlooth.
  20 Lines a Day.
ROBERT L. MCLAUGHLIN, ED.,
  Innovations: An Anthology of Modern &
  Contemporary Fiction.
STEVEN MILLHAUSER, *The Barnum Museum.*
  In the Penny Arcade.
RALPH J. MILLS, JR., *Essays on Poetry.*
OLIVE MOORE, *Spleen.*
NICHOLAS MOSLEY, *Accident.*
  Assassins.
  Catastrophe Practice.
  Children of Darkness and Light.
  The Hesperides Tree.
  Hopeful Monsters.
  Imago Bird.
  Impossible Object.
  Inventing God.
  Judith.
  Look at the Dark.
  Natalie Natalia.
  Serpent.
  The Uses of Slime Mould: Essays of Four Decades.
WARREN F. MOTTE, JR.,
  Fables of the Novel: French Fiction since 1990.
  Oulipo: A Primer of Potential Literature.
YVES NAVARRE, *Our Share of Time.*
DOROTHY NELSON, *Tar and Feathers.*
WILFRIDO D. NOLLEDO, *But for the Lovers.*
FLANN O'BRIEN, *At Swim-Two-Birds.*
  At War.
  The Best of Myles.
  The Dalkey Archive.
  Further Cuttings.
  The Hard Life.
  The Poor Mouth.
  The Third Policeman.
CLAUDE OLLIER, *The Mise-en-Scène.*
PATRIK OUŘEDNÍK, *Europeana.*
FERNANDO DEL PASO, *Palinuro of Mexico.*
ROBERT PINGET, *The Inquisitory.*
  Mahu or The Material.
  Trio.
RAYMOND QUENEAU, *The Last Days.*
  Odile.
  Pierrot Mon Ami.
  Saint Glinglin.
ANN QUIN, *Berg.*
  Passages.
  Three.
  Tripticks.
ISHMAEL REED, *The Free-Lance Pallbearers.*
  The Last Days of Louisiana Red.
  Reckless Eyeballing.
  The Terrible Threes.
  The Terrible Twos.
  Yellow Back Radio Broke-Down.
JULIÁN RÍOS, *Larva: A Midsummer Night's Babel.*
  Poundemonium.
AUGUSTO ROA BASTOS, *I the Supreme.*
JACQUES ROUBAUD, *The Great Fire of London.*

Hortense in Exile.
Hortense Is Abducted.
The Plurality of Worlds of Lewis.
The Princess Hoppy.
Some Thing Black.
LEON S. ROUDIEZ, *French Fiction Revisited.*
VEDRANA RUDAN, *Night.*
LYDIE SALVAYRE, *The Company of Ghosts.*
  The Lecture.
LUIS RAFAEL SÁNCHEZ, *Macho Camacho's Beat.*
SEVERO SARDUY, *Cobra & Maitreya.*
NATHALIE SARRAUTE, *Do You Hear Them?*
  Martereau.
  The Planetarium.
ARNO SCHMIDT, *Collected Stories.*
  Nobodaddy's Children.
CHRISTINE SCHUTT, *Nightwork.*
GAIL SCOTT, *My Paris.*
JUNE AKERS SEESE,
  Is This What Other Women Feel Too?
  What Waiting Really Means.
AURELIE SHEEHAN, *Jack Kerouac Is Pregnant.*
VIKTOR SHKLOVSKY, *Knight's Move.*
  A Sentimental Journey: Memoirs 1917-1922.
  Theory of Prose.
  Third Factory.
  Zoo, or Letters Not about Love.
JOSEF ŠKVORECKÝ,
  The Engineer of Human Souls.
CLAUDE SIMON, *The Invitation.*
GILBERT SORRENTINO, *Aberration of Starlight.*
  Blue Pastoral.
  Crystal Vision.
  Imaginative Qualities of Actual Things.
  Mulligan Stew.
  Pack of Lies.
  The Sky Changes.
  Something Said.
  Splendide-Hôtel.
  Steelwork.
  Under the Shadow.
W. M. SPACKMAN, *The Complete Fiction.*
GERTRUDE STEIN, *Lucy Church Amiably.*
  The Making of Americans.
  A Novel of Thank You.
PIOTR SZEWC, *Annihilation.*
STEFAN THEMERSON, *Hobson's Island.*
  Tom Harris.
JEAN-PHILIPPE TOUSSAINT, *Television.*
ESTHER TUSQUETS, *Stranded.*
DUBRAVKA UGRESIC, *Lend Me Your Character.*
  Thank You for Not Reading.
MATI UNT, *Things in the Night.*
LUISA VALENZUELA, *He Who Searches.*
BORIS VIAN, *Heartsnatcher.*
PAUL WEST, *Words for a Deaf Daughter & Gala.*
CURTIS WHITE, *America's Magic Mountain.*
  The Idea of Home.
  Memories of My Father Watching TV.
  Monstrous Possibility: An Invitation to
  Literary Politics.
  Requiem.
DIANE WILLIAMS, *Excitability: Selected Stories.*
  Romancer Erector.
DOUGLAS WOOLF, *Wall to Wall.*
  Ya! & John-Juan.
PHILIP WYLIE, *Generation of Vipers.*
MARGUERITE YOUNG, *Angel in the Forest.*
  Miss MacIntosh, My Darling.
REYOUNG, *Unbabbling.*
ZORAN ŽIVKOVIĆ, *Hidden Camera.*
LOUIS ZUKOFSKY, *Collected Fiction.*
SCOTT ZWIREN, *God Head.*

FOR A FULL LIST OF PUBLICATIONS, VISIT:
w w w . d a l k e y a r c h i v e . c o m